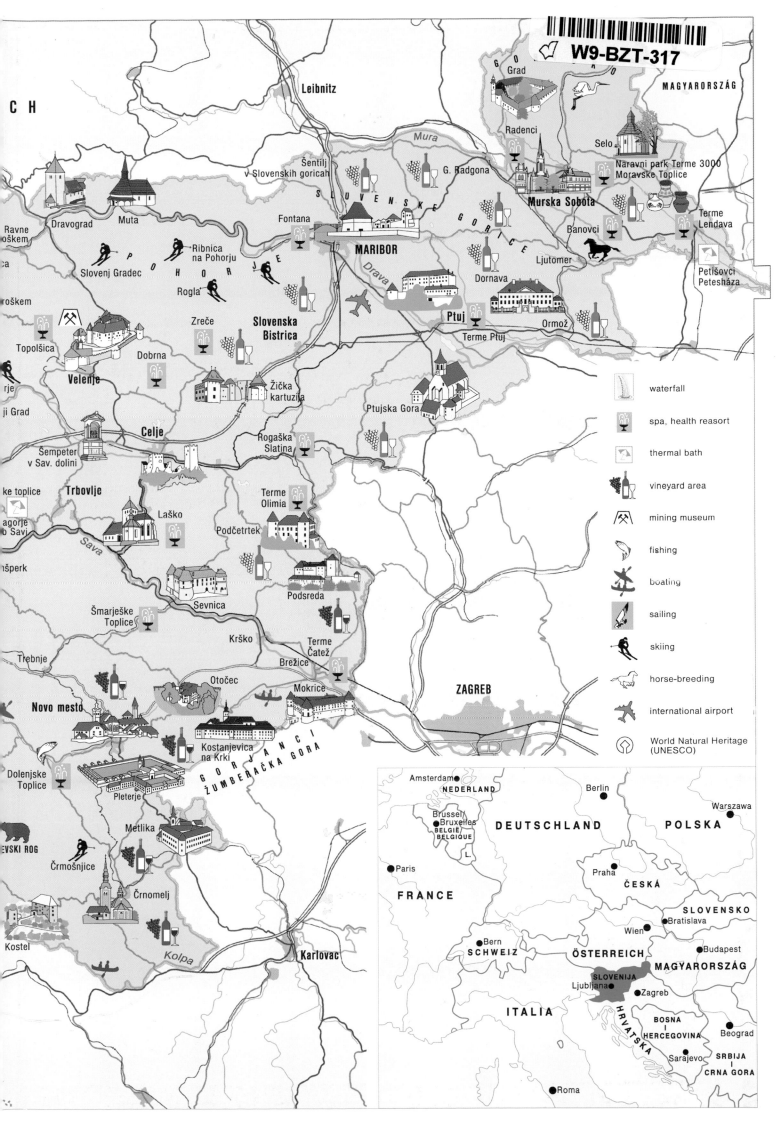

W9-BZT-317

MAGYARORSZÁG

Leibnitz

Mura

Grad

Radenci

Selo

Naravni park Terme 3000
Moravske Toplice

Šentilj
v Slovenskih goricah

Fontana

G. Radgona

SLOVENSKE

GORICE

Murska Sobota

Terme
Lendava

Banovci

Dravograd

Muta

Ribnica
na Pohorju

MARIBOR

Drava

Ljutomer

Petišovci
Petesháza

Ravne
oškem

POHORJE

Slovenj Gradec

Rogla

Dornava

ca

roškem

Zreče

Slovenska
Bistrica

Ptuj

Ormož

Topolšica

Dobrna

Žička
kartuzija

Ptujska Gora

Terme Ptuj

rje

Velenje

ji Grad

Celje

Šempeter
v Sav. dolini

Rogaška
Slatina

ke toplice

Trbovlje

Laško

Terme
Olimia

agorje
b Savi

Sava

Podčetrtek

nšperk

Šmarješke
Toplice

Podsreda

Trebnje

Sevnica

Krško

Terme
Čatež

Brežice

ZAGREB

Otočec

Mokrice

Novo mesto

Kostanjevica
na Krki

GORJANCI

ŽUMBERAČKA GORA

Dolenjske
Toplice

Pleterje

EVSKI ROG

Metlika

Črmošnjice

Črnomelj

Kostel

Kolpa

Karlovac

	waterfall
	spa, health reasort
	thermal bath
	vineyard area
	mining museum
	fishing
	boating
	sailing
	skiing
	horse-breeding
	international airport
	World Natural Heritage (UNESCO)

Amsterdam

NEDERLAND

Berlin

Warszawa

Brussel
Bruxelles
BELGIË
BELGIQUE

DEUTSCHLAND

POLSKA

L.

Paris

Praha

ČESKÁ

FRANCE

SLOVENSKO

Bratislava

Bern

Wien

SCHWEIZ

ÖSTERREICH

Budapest

MAGYARORSZÁG

SLOVENIJA

Ljubljana

Zagreb

ITALIA

HRVATSKA

BOSNA
I
HERCEGOVINA

Beograd

Sarajevo

SRBIJA
I
CRNA GORA

Roma

Greetings from Slovenia

Mladinska knjiga
ZALOŽBA

Contents

Slovenia is a crossroads of nations, a crossroads squeezed between the dominating Alps and the humble Pannonian Plain. Native Slovenes return home after years of exile, some after months of study or weeks of job, all with a burning heart. Foreigners come to meet new friends, to consolidate old ties, to sign contracts. Or – those who appreciate this green garden of Europe – to listen to the silence of mountain lakes, to see the glory of sunrise and sunset on high summits, or to compete with the waves of the Adriatic.

The roar of aircraft at the Brnik airport is stifled by gusts of wind from the high slopes of the Grintovci. A short drive to the east is Slovenia's capital, Ljubljana, and to the west a fairy-tale island dwarfed by the cliff-hanging castle of Bled. A short distance to the south, you can hear the chatter of Piran's Slovene-Italians on their afternoon stroll. At the opposite corner of this land spread the groves of the lower Ledava plain, where the west wind sweeps across the Slovene-Hungarian border.

The almost eight kilometre tunnel through the Karavanke is the world's 14th longest tunnel. It is Slovenia's latest and brightest gateway to the world. The tunnel not only shortens the already short distances within Slovenia, but also makes Europe as a whole much more readily accessible.

The very top of the 2864-metre high Triglav, who rubs shoulders with other majestic Alpine summits, is perched above a precipitous thousand-metre-high north face. From this truly majestic mountain, the eye catches the blue reflection of the Adriatic Sea in the Gulf of Trieste, and to the east, the contours of the Slovene-Croatian Gorjanci range.

But let's get a good view of the land from ground level. Let's have fun recounting statistics; let's follow the descriptions of tranquil lakes and silenced mills by the river, of castles and solitary farmsteads, of karst caves and virgin forests, of traces of the distant past, and of Slovenia's natural and cultural heritage. Let's take a moment and savour the images of a country in its Sunday best and its everyday clothes.

Marjan Krušič

Profile of Slovenia

In a plebiscite in December 1990 the people of Slovenia voted overwhelmingly for independence. Following the proclamation of sovereignty of the Republic of Slovenia on June 25, 1991 and a ten-day-war against the Yugoslav Army, the country was recognised by most of the international community in January 1992. In May of the same year Slovenia became a member of the United Nations Organisation. The country now is a pluralist, parliamentary democracy; Slovenia's national anthem reflects the country's democratic nature and its peaceful system:

God's blessing on all nations,
Who long and work for that bright day,
When o'er earth's habitations
No war, no strife shall hold its sway;
Who long to see
That all men free
No more shall foes, but neighbours be.

The national anthem is the seventh verse of France Prešeren's poem *Zdravljica* (A Toast), set to music by Stanko Premrl

Slovenia is a small country in Central Europe. It lies on the south-eastern side of the Alps, where the Mediterranean and south-east Europe meet. Few places in the world can pride themselves on such a variety of landscape as Slovenia with its area of only 20,273 km² (56.5 % is forest) at the junction of some of Europe's major geographical divides. From the north and north-west the high Alps (the Karavanke, Julian Alps, Kamnik-Savinja Alps) extend into Slovenia, including the highest summit, Triglav (2,864 m), the world-famous Planica, the valley of the ski jumps, and two of nature's finest gems – Lake Bled and Lake Bohinj. Eastwards the Alps gradually settle into the vineyard hills on the fringes of the Pannonian basin; the tectonic faults of the area gave birth to most of Slovenia's spas. Towards the south the Alps descend into the karstic and forested Dinaric Alps, which stretch out along the Adriatic coast and deep into the heartland of the Balkan peninsula. The Slovene section of the Dinaric range is the centre of the country's most-frequented tourist caves (the Postojna Cave, the Škocjan Caves), with Lipica, the home of the Slovene breed of white horses – the Lippizaner. A small, but precious pocket of Slovenia lies on the Adriatic Sea; here, the sub-Mediterranean hills of Slovene Istria are wedged between the coast and the high edge of the Kras (Karst), and the coast features strikingly Mediterranean architecture in Koper/Capodistria, Izola/Isola and Piran/Pirano, as well as in the modern tourist centre Portorož/Portorose. All the principal traffic connections between individual provinces meet in the centrally located capital of Ljubljana.

Slovene flag and coat-of-arms

Left: Piran/Pirano

The Heart of Slovenia
Ljubljana and its environs

The southern part of the Ljubljana basin is the meeting point of three large geographical regions: the Alpine, the pre-Alpine and the Dinaric. This area has been an important crossroads as early as in prehistory. Routes leading to the Eastern Alps, the Pannonian Plain and the northern Adriatic passed through this crossroads. The Ljubljana Gate was a key point of passage on a route running from the south-west to the north-east, which traversed the marshlands of Ljubljansko Barje and the plain of Ljubljansko polje. The other line of communication runs at right angles to the first, following the Sava River. In ancient times a route linked the eastern edge of Ljubljansko Barje with Dolenjska (Lower Carniola) and continued due south-west. The old navigable waterway on the Sava and the Ljubljanica reached as far as Vrhnika, which gives the ancient myth of the Argonauts, the adventurous Greek sailors who stole the Golden Fleece and looked for a passage from the Danube basin to the Adriatic Sea, an element of credibility.

The lower part of the Ljubljana basin is wedged between two hill ranges. From the south-east, the Posavje hills, with Golovec and the Castle Hill (Grajski hrib) jut into the Ljubljana basin; from the opposite side, the Polhov Gradec mountain range extends to the fringes of Ljubljana. The Ljubljana basin is thus sharply divided into two very different areas: the Ljubljansko Barje and the Ljubljansko polje.

The marshy plain south of Ljubljana was given its present name in the 19th century. Its appearance has changed considerably in the past two centuries. Before drainage works were undertaken in the late 18th century, vast layers of peat covered the marshlands, the largest such deposits in the Austrian Empire, which provided a haven for rare and fascinating wildlife. In several places the peat layer attained a thickness of 8 metres, but later, mainly before the First World War, it was depleted. As the marshes began disappearing, many rare plants and animals, indigenous to this area of Slovenia, also vanished. Geologically, Ljubljansko Barje is a young tectonic depression. Considerable subsidence occurred during the last Ice Age, and it seems that this process is still alive today, even though it is much slower.

1 The old centre of Ljubljana has completely preserved its historical core, wedged between the foot of the Castle Hill and the Ljubljanica. Its banks, where small boats once used to unload goods, were turned into promenades after the river was regulated in the 1908–32 period. Čevljarski most (Shoemaker's Bridge, architect Plečnik) and a wooden footbridge connect the promenades.

Left: Ljubljana's centre with the Ljubljanica and the Castle Hill
Below: Location of aerial photograph shown on map 1 : 300 000

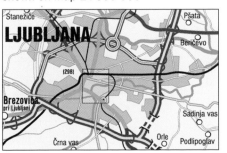

2

5

3

6

4

2 Ancient Roman Emona was the first town located at the strategically important Ljubljana Gate. Its role of crossroads was inherited by Ljubljana. The sculpture of a Roman notable (the *Emonian*) is an exquisite archaeological find from the Roman era.

3 This memorial to the general and poet Rudolf Maister, who secured the northern border of Slovenia after the First World War, stands on Trg Osvobodilne fronte (Liberation Front Square) across the railway station.

4 Town Hall, Robba's Fountain, and the cathedral of St. Nicholas are among the town's most picturesque sights.

5 Cankarjev dom (Cankar Centre), Slovenia's biggest cultural centre, is of recent vintage. Together with the buildings of Ljubljanska banka (Ljubljana Bank) and the Emona-Maximarket department store it forms the largest cultural and business complex in the country. A memorial to the writer Ivan Cankar stands at the entrance to Cankarjev dom.

6 The Seminary dates from the first decade of the 18th century and houses the oldest public library in Ljubljana. The illusionist frescoes on the library's vault are from 1721.

7 The door-handle at the main entrance to the National and University Library, designed by the architect Jože Plečnik.

The hills of Ljubljansko Barje, such as Kostanjevica, Plešivica and Babna gorica, are simply the peaks of former hills which have been submerged in the marshland. Rivers and streams filled the depression with gravel and other alluvial deposits, and when the process of subsidence outpaced the process of alluvial deposition, a lake was formed. The last lake inhabited by so-called lake dwellers disappeared several thousand years ago.

Ljubljansko Barje is one of the oldest settled locations in the Ljubljana basin and the whole of central Slovenia. It was inhabited towards the end of the Middle Ice Age (microlithic culture) and later at the end of the Late Stone Age, as well as at the dawn of the Copper Age (pile-dwelling culture). On the southern fringes of the marshlands, near Ig, nine communities of lake dwellers have been discovered, dating back from the end of the Neolithic to the Early Bronze Age. The Iron Age settlements were built on solid ground, mainly on elevated, well-protected, strategic sites in the form of forts. The Roman period brought the first town-like settlement, at first a military outpost and later also a civilian settlement called Emona. It was built on a plain above the Ljubljanica, at the point where the Castle Hill and Rožnik come closest to each other. The Romans built the first roads and regulated the banks of the Ljubljanica from Emona to its source at Nauportus (Vrhnika). When the Roman Empire crumbled, Emona also disappeared. Medieval Ljubljana is first mentioned as Laybach in 1144, and in 1146 as Luwigana. The community was granted municipal rights in 1220. Unlike Emona, the medieval settlement hugged the foot of the Castle Hill on the right bank of the Ljubljanica. Initially it was a minor town of lesser importance than Kranj or Kamnik, but as it grew, it became an increasingly important urban center, and in the middle of the 13th century, the capital of Carniola. In the 18th and 19th centuries, when Slovene nationalism was sweeping across the land, Ljubljana became a cultural centre, and with the founding of Yugoslavia in 1918, it also became the administrative centre of Slovenia. From 26th June 1991 Ljubljana became the capital of the newly sovereign Republic of Slovenia.

To the north and east of Ljubljana sprawls the fertile plain of Ljubljansko polje, a genuine contrast to the Marshes. In fact, this is a broadened section of the valley of the Sava. The Sava and its tributaries (the largest of which is the Kamniška Bistrica) filled the basin with glacial debris. The thick gravel deposits store large quantities of high-quality drinking water which supply the city of Ljubljana. The Sava has a considerable gradient and runs quite swiftly. Its river bed has been cut through gravel deposits, which allow the river to change its course quite often. Whenever the waters of the Sava encounter bedrock, they turn into rapids. The Ljubljanica, on the other hand, has almost no gradient as far as Ljubljana, flowing at a leisurely pace. Its bed cuts through clay deposits, and at high water the river spills over its banks and floods Ljubljansko Barje.

Just as the ancient routes were unable to do, more recent transportation facilities could not bypass the Ljubljana basin. The first railway in Slovenia linked Vienna with Trieste, reaching Ljubljana in 1849. Later, constructors encountered many problems in traversing Ljubljansko Barje. Of particular interest was the viaduct at Borovnica, a masterful piece of civil engineering. By the end of the 19th century Ljubljana had become a railway centre, with rail links to Carinthia, Zagreb and Trieste, and local destinations in Dolenjska, Kamnik, and Vrhnika (the latter has been abandoned). The recently constructed motorways now connect Ljubljana with the regions of Primorska, Dolenjska and Gorenjska.

8 A part of Tivoli, Ljubljana's biggest park, and Tivoli Mansion, once Podturn Castle.

9 Double-peaked Šmarna gora (Šmarna gora proper 669 m, Grmada 676 m) is the most frequented hill in all of Slovenia. A nature trail is laid out across the hill. The hilltop is the site of the Church of Our Lady, surrounded by a medieval wall, and is part of the Slovene Geological Path.

10 Ljubljana Airport at Brnik, one of Slovenia's three international airports, is set against the majestic scenery of the Karavanke and the Kamnik Alps.

11 The alluvial deposits of the Sora, Sava, Kamniška Bistrica, and Pšata rivers are covered by vast, fertile fields.

12 The Ljubljana Marshes are the vast wetland plain south of Ljubljana. From around 2300 to 1700 BC pile dwellings existed in the area, which was then covered by a lake. The past two centuries have seen many attempts to turn this former peat bog into fields, and many have failed. Today the area is of particular value as the habitat of endangered water and marsh birds. In the background the sprawling Krim hill range.

13 The Carthusian monastery at Bistra was erected at the strong karst springs of the same name on the edge of the Ljubljana Marshes in 1255. The buildings now house the Technical Museum of Slovenia. A nature trail is laid out in the forest across the road.

12

13

Over Hill and Dale

The Bača Valley, Cerkno, Idrija and Škofja Loka regions, the Rovte and Polhov Gradec Hills

The Julian Alps and the Jelovica plateau with Ratitovec (1,678 m), its southern side, are flanked by alpine foothills called Cerkljansko-Škofjeloško hribovje (Cerkno-Škofja Loka hills). This is a territory of steep slopes, deep valleys and innumerable ravines traversed by the continental divide of the Adriatic and the Black Sea, which at the local level separates the area into the Cerkno-Idrija and Škofja Loka-Polhov Gradec districts.

This rather rugged territory is largely the result of considerable tectonic activity. Two types of rock predominate: Paleozoic slates and sandstones and Carboniferous and Permian rocks, as well as more recent rocks such as limestones and dolomites of the Triassic period, which make up most of the peaks. In some places, particularly in the hills of Polhov Gradec, erosion has produced characteristic sharp-edged formations. These unique natural features gave rise to the not entirely suitable 'tourist' name of Polhov Gradec Dolomites, a term discouraged by experts.

In terms of geological diversity, this region has no parallel in Slovenia. The fact that this is an orographic meeting point and a tectonically active region is borne out by the Idrija fault line, which is quite clearly visible on the map and is seen even better in a satellite photograph. It runs in an almost straight line from the Taglimento in Friuli, via Tolmin and Idrija, to Čabar. The fault line was formed by the so-called Adriatic tectonic plate embedded under the European continental crust, according to geologists. At the mine in Idrija a displacement of 60 cm has been recorded over the last six decades. Occasionally, powerful earthquakes occur along this fault line, such as the rather recent tremors which rocked the Tolmin area in 1976, and the Bovec basin in 1998. But the most catastrophic quake, with its epicentre in Idrija, occurred in 1511. This was one of the worst earthquakes in the history of Slovenia, destroying a large part of the affected area. Fortunately, Idrija was at the time a young mining town with mainly wooden structures, because its rich deposits of mercury ore had been discovered only a short time before the quake. After the earthquake Idrija developed into an important economic and cultural center of this rather remote region. Employment in the imperial mine attracted people from near and far. The town also attracted many renowned

1 The village of Rut above the Bača Valley has a long and fascinating history. It dates back to the 13th century when it was established by German immigrants (its old name is Nemški – *German* – Rut). The old linden in front of the church (circumference: 795 cm) witnesses to the ancient tradition of village self-rule.

Left: Zgornja Sorica (The Upper Sorica village) above the Selca Valley
Below: Location of aerial photograph shown on map 1 : 300 000

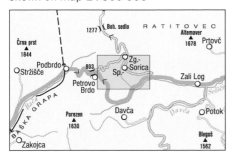

2 Cerkno nestles in a picturesque small hollow below Porezen

3 The Franja Partisan Field Hospital, hidden deep in the almost impracticable Pasica ravine near the village of Dolenji Novaki, was constructed in total secrecy. It welcomed the first wounded partisans on December 23, 1943, and by the end of the war a total of 522 partisans had been treated there. The hospital was named after the partisan doctor Dr. Franja Bojc-Bidovec.

4 Divje jezero (Wild Lake) near Idrija is a karst spring, set in an enticing environment. In 1967 the spring was protected as a natural monument, and in 1972 the environment was arranged as an open-air museum. In 1993 it was included in the landscape park of the Idrijca in Belca rivers. With its 55-metre course, the Jezernica, which flows into the Idrijca, is the shortest river in Slovenia.

5 Idrija is the oldest mining town in Slovenia and a traditional lace centre. A part of the mine has been arranged for tourist visits, and the Gewerkenegg Castle, once the seat of the mine's management, now houses the collections of the Municipal Museum.

6 This former miners' house on a slope above the Frančiška mine was turned into a museum.

7 Lace-making was supposedly introduced in Idrija in the 16th century by the wives of Bohemian miners, from there it spread to Ljubljana, Cerkno, and the valleys of Selca and Poljane.

scientists, who came to Idrija to conduct research and in the process became permanent members of the history of Slovene science. Some of the most notable were I. A. Scopoli, J. Mrak, B. Hacquet, F. Hladnik, H. Freyer, and D. Dežman. The history of the mining period is retained in the Mining Museum, part of the Municipial Museum, which was awarded the Luigi Micheletti prize as the best technical European Museum of 1997.

The mining industry was not restricted to Idrija. A long time before Idrija's mining boom, iron ore was being mined and turned into iron in the Škofja Loka region. An old blast furnace at Železniki is a reminder of those times. Slate for roofing was cut at Zali Log and Dolenja vas in the Selca Valley and there are still many such slate roofs. Under Blegoš in the Poljane Valley, banded limestone is quarried, known as Hotavlje marble. In 1991 low profitability and respect of the environment closed down Slovenia's only uranium mine at Žirovski vrh.

Divje jezero (Wild Lake), a fascinating karst formation, lies near the upper flow of the Idrijca in a deep, rock-bound cauldron. The lake is fed by a deep subterranean stream, and divers have still not reached its bottom. So far, some 250 metres of its length have been swum, and the deepest dive was to 83 metres. The lake also feeds the Idrijca. The Divje babe cave, above the Idrijca bed and the settlement of Reka, is an interesting archeological site, providing evidence that the Neanderthals lived there 45,000 years ago.

The history of the Škofja Loka region began in 973 when the region passed into the hands of the Bavarian bishops of Freising, who built their administrative center at the confluence of the Selška Sora and the Poljanska Sora. Škofja Loka is one of Slovenia's oldest towns and has to this day preserved the authentic appearance of the old town reconstructed after the 1511 earthquake. During the 800 years of rule by the Freising bishops, many Germans came to this area, mostly to work on the land, and were eventually assimilated into the Slovene population.

At the foot of Polhograjska gora, the site of a fortified settlement in prehistoric and ancient times, lies Polhov Gradec. In 1837, the town achieved European renown thanks to a local nobleman, Rihard Blagay, who found on the mountain an unidentified species of daphne, which was named in his honor *Daphne blagayana*.

The Idrija and Cerkno regions are dotted with many monuments dedicated to the memory of the Second World War, and testimonies to the extraordinary human and cultural dimensions of Slovenia's national liberation struggle: the partisan hospitals called Pavla and Franja, and the Slovenija print shop. Thanks to the well-concealed location of these facilities and support by the local population, the enemy never discovered them.

Nowhere in Slovenia can cultivated fields be found on such steep slopes, nor human dwellings in such remote location as in the regions of Idrija and Cerkno. The building methods are also quite peculiar. The Idrija houses with massive walls and several storeys are set up at right angles against the slopes (not parallel to the slopes). Villages and solitary hamlets also dot the mountains of Škofja Loka.

The village of Davča is reputedly the most extended community of Slovenia, with solitary homesteads reaching up to 1,120 metres. Many old roads have been modernized and many of the hamlets are now linked to the rest of the world.

8

9

10

11

12

8 Historically, the village of Poljane nad Škofjo Loko was the most important settlement in the Poljane Valley. The valley and the river's right fork, the Poljane Sora (Poljanščica) were named after it. Poljane occupies the left bank of the Sora, Hotavlje the right one.

9 Though damaged by a fire, this mighty chestnut tree, 27 m high and with a circumference of 1005 cm at breast height, grows near the Zejčar homestead on a slope of Gabrška gora above the Poljane Valley.

10 The idyllic church of St. Primus dominates the high ridge near the settlement of Jamnik between Kropa and Dražgoše. The view from the ridge captures the Karavanke and the entire Radovljica basin.

11 Žiri consists of several villages and today's centre is the former independent village of Stara vas. The settlement is renowned for its modern shoe industry and traditional lace. The highest building is the two-tower church of St. Martin from 1906.

12 The church of the Annunciation at Crngrob has a Late Romanesque layout from the 13th century, which was adapted in the Gothic style in the 15th century. The church was decorated with wall paintings on the inside and outside, and it has one of the richest 17th-century gilded altars in Slovenia.

13 Idrija, Žiri, Vrhnika, and Logatec more or less form the borders of the undulating Rovte hills. The highest hill is Vrh svetih Treh kraljev ("The Mount of the Magi", 884 m), which offers splendid views.

14 This Baroque mansion stands in a narrow valley near Polhov Gradec and the Neptune fountain in front of it is the biggest one in Slovenia. Nearby Gora is known for its habitats of Blagay's Daphne *(Daphne blagayana),* an endemic plant named after Count Ursini-Blagay, the lord of the manor of Polhov Gradec.

15 Over a thousand years old, Škofja Loka, located on the confluence of the Selca Sora and the Poljane Sora, has an exceptionally well preserved medieval urban core around Mestni trg (Town Square). A castle, which houses the Loka Museum, towers over the town.

13

14

15

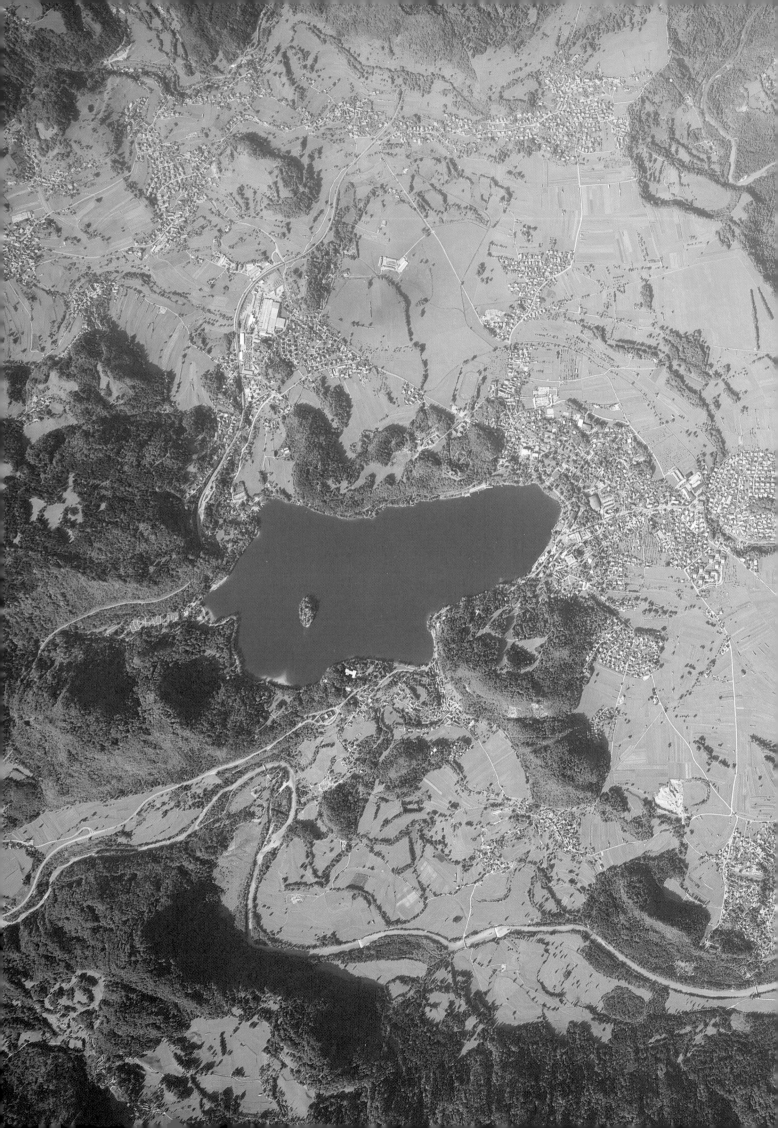

Between the Julian Alps and the Karavanke

Planica, the Upper Sava Valley, Bled, Radovljica and Kranj plains

1 The Planica valley under the Poncas, which, with its head called Tamar, cuts deep under Jalovec, is a centre of ski jumps and ski flying. All the important world records were set here: the 100- and 200-metre marks were surpassed for the first time in human history (Sepp Bradl, 101 m, in 1936, and Toni Nieminen, 203 m, in 1994), and in 2003, Matti Hautamäki reached 231 m.

Left: Bled and its environs
Below: Location of aerial photograph shown on map 1 : 300 000

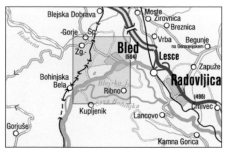

Millions of years ago, in the Tertiary period, when the Alps began to acquire their present appearance, a powerful tectonic fault separated the present-day Julian Alps from the Karavanke and the Kamnik Alps. The sloping fault line can be followed from the Kokra to Rateče and further on across the frontier into Italy. This natural dividing line is today called Zgornjesavska dolina (the Upper Sava Valley).

The source of the Sava is at Zelenci near Podkoren, where the underground waters from the Planica valley come to light. At first, the spring has no gradient and stagnates in a marsh. This unusual natural habitat between Rateče and Podkoren abounds in rare plants and animals, and is the true source of the Sava Dolinka, the northern fork of the Sava. The first 221 kilometres of its total length of 947 kilometres make the Sava the longest river in Slovenia. It runs across the whole territory and into the Republic of Croatia.

Since pre-historic times, the Upper Sava Valley has been an important commercial route linking the Gorenjska and Koroška regions. The pass at Rateče provides the lowest-lying Alpine passage (853 m above sea level) from the Sava Valley to the Kanal and Drava valleys. Here, the first Gorenjska railway line was built in 1870, connecting the towns of Ljubljana and Tarvisio. In the Middle Ages, this principal route was challenged by a cargo route to Carinthia by way of the Koren and Ljubelj passes. It was not until 1906 that a railway line from the Karavanke to Bohinj, running north to south, linked Bohinj with the rest of the world. The Vršič road, built in 1916, connected the Sava and Soča valleys. The latest transportation facility is the 7864-metre long Karavanke tunnel (road), running parallel to that of 1906 (railway).

At Žirovnica, the valley suddenly opens up into a broad plain consisting of the western part of the Ljubljana basin fringed by the Karavanke range and the southern slopes of the Kamnik Alps in the north and east, and the Jelovica plateau with Bled in the south. The Radovljica plain was once a deep valley of the Sava, but was later, during the Ice Age, filled with moraines and alluvial deposits. The Sava cut a new river bed through these gravel deposits, in places consolidated into conglomerate stone.

▶

2 Zelenci, a picturesque area with a rich biodiversity, includes the headwaters of the Sava Dolinka and numerous springs between Rateče and Podkoren.

3 Predominantly a holiday resort, Kranjska Gora is located in the scenic mountain environment of the Karavanke and Julian Alps. Its tourist assets include ski areas, indoor swimming pools in the hotels, numerous walking paths, easy access to the Vršič pass, and a casino. The summits in the background are those of Razor and Prisank.

4 The Liznjek house in Kranjska Gora dates from the late 18th century and was turned into a museum.

5 The mountains of the Martuljek Group are among the most picturesque scenes in the Julian Alps. The Martuljek stream, which flows out of the Za Akom cirque, forms two falls on its way down. The top one is 50 m high.

6 The 19th century saw the decline of the smiths's craft at Kropa, but was soon replaced by the decorative iron art.

Two natural wonders of Slovenia are the result of the Bohinj glacier, extending all the way into the Radovljica basin. The first is Lake Bled, which formed at the bottom of the former glacier, featuring the only true island in the whole of Slovenia. The other natural wonder is the Vintgar gorge. The glacier formed a barrier for the Radovna, which had flowed past Bled into the Sava. A larger lake formed in the valley. All that remains of the former lake is cretaceous sediments at Srednja Radovna. When the water level was high enough, the water between the hills of Hom and Boršt spilled into the Sava Valley. Over millennia, the Radovna carved out the picturesque gap called Vintgar, through which the Radovna lake slowly seeped out. What remains today is a fine natural sight.

The valleys of the Gorenjska region were inhabited quite early. At Drulovka near Kranj, a settlement from the Late Stone Age has been discovered, and at Bled, Bronze Age finds testify to human presence. Since then, people and their cultural development have been continuously present in this area. In the Early Iron Age or the Hallstatt period, iron was forged here. An ore called *bobovec* was found in Jelovica, Pokljuka and in the vicinity of Jesenice. The iron-making tradition continued through the medieval period and flourished from the 15th to 17th centuries in the Selca Valley, Bohinj, Radovna, Jesenice and all the way to Mojstrana. Today, iron works are still present in Jesenice and Kropa, although the iron ore deposits were worked out long ago.

Recent archaeological research has shown that Bled with environs was densely populated even at the time of the fall of the Roman Empire and later in the Old Slavonic period. The Slovenes settled the Castle Hill, the shores of Lake Bled and the island. There may be some truth to the legend of a temple dedicated to the goddess Živa described in France Prešerns's poem. In 1004 a deed of land signed by Henry II granting Bled and its environs to the Brixen bishops contains the first mention of Bled Castle, which is also one of the oldest castles in Slovenia.

In the Middle Ages, the town of Kranj and the borough of Radovljica increasingly took on the role of administrative centres owing to their favourable strategic location. Gorenjska, the central and the most important area in Carniola, continues its historical tradition. Its Alpine landscape provides a magnificent natural backdrop for its ancient towns. Quaint traditional Alpine architecture is still found in the villages around Bohinj, at Jezersko, and in the upper reaches of the Sava Dolinka (Upper Sava).

In the north-east of the Radovljica basin, on the sun-kissed Alpine foothills, where the Draga Valley becomes a plain, near the medieval castle fortress of Kamen stands the village of Begunje. During the war, its 17th-century manor housed a Gestapo torture chamber where many Slovenes were killed. Today, Elan, the maker of sports equipment carries the name of Begunje and Slovenia around the globe.

The need for modern traffic connections between Central Europe and the Balkans has resulted in the construction of new roads, such as the motorway through the Karavanke tunnel, passing through Hrušica, the Sava Valley and Ljubljana and continuing to the south.

7 Memorial to the priest, composer, and mountaineering pioneer Jakob Aljaž, who had a turret, named after him, erected on the summit of Triglav in 1895.

8 Završnica, a small hidden valley at the foot of Stol, separates the Karavanke from Brezniške peči, the westernmost outcrop of the Kamnik Alps. In 1915, the Završnica hydro power plant started to operate here, the first public power plant in Slovenia. Its small reservoir has long since blended with the landscape.

9 Some ten thousand years ago the Radovna river cut its way to the Sava Dolinka, carving out the 1,5-km-long and in places 150-m-deep Vintgar gorge, which ends in the 13-m-high Šum waterfall.

10 Draga near Begunje in Gorenjska is the scene of the striking ruins of the medieval Kamen defence castle; nearby is the cemetery of 1282 hostages, victims of the Second World War.

11 In 1854 the Swiss Arnold Rikli opened a water-and-air health resort in Bled, and the little town has been the leading holiday resort of Slovenia ever since. The church of the Assumption is exquisitely located on the only lake island in Slovenia, and the castle towering on the high rock above the lake is one of the oldest in the country.

12 A section of the Gothic wall paintings in the church of the Assumption on the island.

11

12

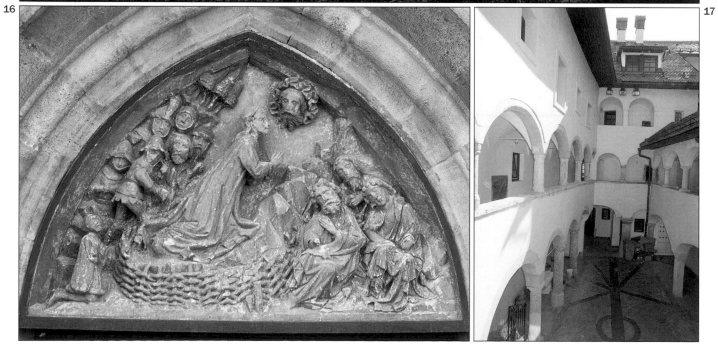

13 The historical centre of Radovljica features several burgher buildings from the 16th and 17th centuries and a lofty Baroque mansion. It is the seat of the Radovljica Municipal Museums, among them the Beekeeping Museum and the A.T. Linhart memorial room.

14 The small Gothic church of St. Mark stands at the edge of the village of Vrba, the native village of the poet France Prešeren. Prešeren's birth-place houses a museum dedicated to the poet.

15 The fertile and colourful Sora plain is a remarkable landscape with characteristic long fields. It was formed by the Sava's rubble deposits and harbours important ground water reserves. In the foreground the flooded Zarica, a gorge carved out by the Sava near the village of Jama.

16 The core of medieval Kranj is dominated by the Gothic church of St. Cantianus. The relief which is preserved above the main portal shows the scene on Mount Olive.

17 The Pavšlar house in Kranj is a precious example of burgher architecture. It grew out of three buildings erected in the 15th century. Its courtyard was surrounded with arcaded corridors in the 16th century.

18 The Sava Dolinka and Sava Bohinjka join in a scenic spot between the foot of Jelovica and a high rock promontory, on which the town of Radovljica is set. In ancient times, the Bohinj glacier extended this far and Obla gorica, a little hill, is a remnant of its terminal moraine.

19 Kranj's origin was an old settlement on a terrace hovering high above the confluence of the Kokra and Sava rivers. As early as the 11th century it was the seat of the Carniolan margrave, and it was granted town privileges in the 13th century.

18

19

The Gardens of Zlatorog

The Julian Alps, Trenta, the Bovec basin, Bohinj, Mežakla, Pokljuka, Jelovica

1 Jalovec (here seen from Sleme) is a conspicuous mountain because of its height (2,645 m) and shape. Its pointed pyramid with the typical notch is visible from the three valleys of Loška Koritnica, Trenta, and Planica. To the left surges Šite's impressive north face above the Tamar valley.

Left: The head of the Triglav Lakes Valley
Below: Location of aerial photograph shown on map 1 : 300 000

At the juncture of the Alps and the Dinaric mountains lie Slovenia's loftiest summits. The mountain range is called the Julian Alps, named after the Roman town of Forum Iulii (present-day Čedad). The town was named after Gaius Julius Caesar.

The Julian Alps consist of carbonate rock, limestone, and dolomites, which were deposited in the Mesozoic era over many millennia on the bottom of the sea. These strata of several thousand metres gradually became dry land as the region was lifted and the sea flowed away. During the transition from the Mesozoic to the Cenozoic, the entire area of the present Alps from the Ligurian sea to the Pannonian Plain was subject to considerable tectonic activity and shifts in the earth's crust. Several major folds were eventually flattened out, while others were overthrust due to pressures from within the crust. An example of the overthrust is the Triglav Lakes Valley, better known to geologists as the Slatna Plate. Today's plateaus of Pokljuka, Komna and Jelovica are probably larger pieces of this plate which have remained relatively consolidated. However, greater pressures on the edges produced crescents of mountain ranges (such as the mountains of Bohinj, Ratitovec, the peaks between Draški vrh and Debela peč on the fringes of Pokljuka, or the Komna range). The highest peaks is Triglav (2,864 m). In places where the rock masses could not withstand the pressure, fractures occurred which further articulated the jagged topography. By the late Tertiary period, the Julian Alps had displayed their present-day profile, but at the same time, weathering began to reshape the surface. Along the fault lines, where the rock was relatively fissured, the Soča, Koritnica, Sava and other rivers carved out valleys, in which lakes appeared and then vanished under rock falls and glaciation.

The Ice Age which began a million years ago also shaped the appearance of the Alps. Of the many glaciers covering a large portion of the Julian Alps, the largest two slid down the Soča and Sava Bohinjka valleys. The ice from the Sava Valley piled up so high that it reached Pokljuka. The glaciers left behind U-shaped valleys, like Bohinj, glacial moraines, solitary boulders, and glacial lakes, ranging from the largest Bohinj lake (4.1 km long and 45 m deep) to the high-altitude Triglav lakes (Triglavska jezera), Krn lakes (Krnska jezera) and Križ lakes (Kriška jezera, the highest lake is 2,160 m above sea level).

2

3

4

2 Vršič (1,611 m) is the best-known Alpine pass in the Julian Alps. The first road across it was constructed by Russian prisoners of war in 1916. 160 to 300 of them paid a terrible price when they were buried by a snow avalanche. In the background Mojstrovka.

3 The memorial Russian chapel from the First World War stands by the road which leads up to the Vršič pass.

4 Škrlatica (2,740 m), or Suhi plaz as it used to be called, is the second highest mountain in Slovenia. This mountain group lies between the Vrata and Krnica valleys, beyond the most frequented mountain paths, and has preserved much of its original wild charm.

5 His Alpine majesty, the ibex.

The continental divide between the Adriatic and the Black Sea runs through the Julian Alps.

In addition to Triglav, Slovenia's highest mountain, there are several other natural wonders in this part of the country. The Bovec basin is the largest plain and the deepest, gravel-filled basin in the heart of Slovenia's Alps. Krn, on the Soča side, measured from the village of Kamno to the peak of Krn, represents the highest relative height in Slovenia (2,040 m). Boka is one of the highest known waterfalls in the whole country (106 m); the road to Mangrtsko sedlo is the highest road access (2,072 m), and the state border on the northern slope of Muzci above the stream of Beli potok marks the westernmost point of Slovene territory (12° 23' east of Greenwich).

Because of specific enviromental conditions, highland plant life differs from that of the lowlands. The Julian Alps, however, have two more distinguishing features in comparison with the Central Alps: firstly, carbonate rock permits a wider variety of plant life; secondly, the region borders on other biogeographical areas. Thus the habitats of Mediterranean and Dinaric plant species reach along the warm valleys far into the Alpine realm. The sheltered, sun-warmed slopes are veritable islands of warmth-loving plants (e.g., the mountainsides of Komarča and Pršivec, the slopes above the Radovna). On the other hand, high-altitude locations and freezing points provide a habitat for plants whose original home was the European north or the distant mountains of Asia. These species have come so far in their attempt to escape the advancing Ice Age. Most interesting, of course, are the plants and animals which have survived or developed only in a very restricted area. These are called endemites.

The most famous endemic plants in the Julian Alps are the *Aconitum angustifolium, Centaurea dicroantha, Cerastium uniflorum, Papaver ernesti-mayeri.* Among the butterflies, the Triglav brown butterfly and the Trenta brown butterfly deserve mention.

People explored the Julian Alps as early as in prehistoric times, first along the Sava and Soča Rivers. Remote Bohinj was settled quite early. Iron Age inhabitants were attracted to this secluded land by rich deposits of iron ore. The famous archaeological find of Ajdovski gradec dates to this period. Mining also brought people to the Upper Soča Valley, but the ore was not abundant there. During the Roman period, the ore deposits in the Soča Valley were depleted and the iron industry died out. Nevertheless, Bohinj iron foundry continued to flourish into modern times. Bohinj was connected with the Soča Valley by way of the Vrh Bače pass. Later it also established firm ties with the Gorenjska region by way of Bled. Around the year 500 an important sacral center at Tonovcov grad developed and remained important even in the Middle Ages. In the late 12th century, most valleys were inhabited and the level land was cultivated. The next step was to populate the higher-lying areas, first the southern slopes of mountains. Forests were cleared for agriculture and grazing. A sharp increase in population in the Middle Ages resulted in the first human forays into the mountains and permanent high-lying settlements, and people began to seek more pastureland at higher elevations, close to the timber line. By the end of the Middle Ages, the Julian Alps were densely populated and experienced the most intensive deforestation. The forests in Trenta, Bohinj, Pokljuka and Jelovica were depleted to provide wood for iron production. Wood for the continuously burning furnaces was in short supply. The soil was destroyed by erosion, and the timber line was lowered by about a hundred metres. When, in the 18th century, the furnaces of Trenta, and in the

▶

6

7

8

6 Triglav and its mighty North Face. No end of wishes, thoughts, yearnings, faith, and strength are personified by this superb national symbol of the Slovenes.

7 And how many devout souls have ascended its summit after the first documented ascent in 1778! Most visitors stop over at Triglavski Dom, the mountain hut located highest in Slovenia, built in 1896 and enlarged to its present size in 1993.

8 The Dvojno jezero (Double Lake) lies halfway up the Triglav Lakes Valley, and here the history of the Triglav National Park started in 1908.

9 The picturesque Mlinarica gorge and its troughs in the Trenta valley can be accessed by a tourist trail. In 1951 they were protected as a natural monument.

10 An old homestead in the Zadnja Trenta valley and behind it the sun-bathed Bavški Grintovec (2,347 m). Abandoned homes in the Trenta valley have been turned into holiday cottages, and most of them have preserved their original appearance, but the pastures and meadows overgrow quickly.

19th century the furnaces of Bohinj, were finally extinguished, many miners and iron workers moved on, but some stayed to take up farming and husbandry. Commerce declined and many trade routes were abandoned.

The 18th century, the classic age of research into nature, brought several world-renowned scientists (e.g. I. A. Scopoli and B. Hacquet) to this part of the Alps. They were the first to describe the nature of the highlands scientifically. Triglav was first climbed in 1778 by a group of local climbers from Bohinj, on the initiative of Žiga (Sigismund) Zois. While in the early days of Alpine exploration, adventurers and researchers were the most frequent visitors, in the late 19th century German supremacy became evident in Alpine mountaineering. In response, the Slovene Alpine Club was established in 1893. Although organized as a tourist organization, it was in fact a cultural and political association which soon became indispensable to Slovene national awakening. The pilgrimage to Triglav, a practice still alive today, meant an almost ritual confirmation of one's affiliation with the motherland and the Slovene nation.

And finally, there is the legend of Zlatorog and his magical Alpine garden. The legend is synonymous with the Julian Alps and takes place in the Triglav National Park. A proposal put forward in 1908 resulted in the founding of a small "Alpine Protection Park" in 1924, which led to the proclamation of a vast area of the Julian Alps as the Triglav National Park in 1961. The pre-war park was the first protected territory in Slovenia. In 1981 the park was expanded to include most of the eastern part of the Julian Alps. With a surface area of 83,807 hectares it is one of the larger European nature reserves.

The story of Zlatorog

It was many centuries ago that the story was first told of Zlatorog, a mysterious white chamois with golden horns. High in the mountains he had a miraculous garden and a retinue of white fairies who helped him guard a vast, hidden treasure. But a greedy mortal wanted to steal Zlatorog's wealth. So he shot Zlatorog, but instantly, there grew from the blood of the mortal wound a miraculous crimson flower – the Triglav rose. This the dying Zlatorog ate and in a flash his life was restored. In righteous anger he flung the mortal into an abyss, ravaged the mountain paradise, and disappeared. His treasure remains hidden below Triglav.

9

10

▶

11 The river basins of the Upper Soča, Sava Dolinka, and Kamniška Bistrica are known for narrow gorges, carved into the limestone and called troughs. The longest troughs are near the village of Soča.

12 The Savica waterfall (78 m) delighted Valentin Vodnik so much that he wrote an ode in its honour, and it inspired France Prešeren to write the poem *Krst pri Savici* (The Baptism at the Savica). The Savica emerges from a karst water cave, fed by the waters of Komna and the Triglav Lakes Valley. During the First World War, a power plant was constructed at the foot of the waterfall to power the military cableway up to the Komna plateau and the narrow-gauge railway connecting Bohinjska Bistrica and Savica.

13 The Peričnik waterfall (52 m high) has a unique feature – a path leading behind the water curtain. Another waterfall, the Upper Peričnik, is located higher. In winter, when the air temperature drops below the freezing point, the entire rock face left and right of the waterfall changes into an icicle "church organ".

14 Bohinj has preserved some original forms
15 of vernacular architecture, among them are the well-known aligned herdsmen's wooden dwellings on the Zajamniki alp and the cluster of double hayracks in Studor.

16 Lake Bohinj is the biggest and deepest lake in Slovenia. On its banks stands the church of St. John the Baptist in Ribčev Laz at Lake Bohinj. The interior and a part of the exterior are decorated with frescoes dating from different periods; the oldest frescoes are from the early 14th century.

17 Two hundred years ago, at the time of Bohinj's iron industry, the Pokljuka plateau was almost treeless. Ore was probably extracted here already in prehistoric times and throughout the Middle Ages. Several names, among them Rudno polje (Ore Field), witness to the activity. A natural phenomenon of the plateau, which today is part of the Triglav National Park, are its peat bogs and their rare plant species.

The Soča Basin
The Soča Valley, Breginj, the Tolmin region, Banjšice, Brda

1 Sculpture of the mountaineer, writer, and researcher Dr. Julius Kugy in Trenta. Kugy popularized the Trenta Valley, its people, and the Julian Alps.

Left: Most na Soči with the Idrijca-Bača and the Soča (dammed)-Idrijca confluences
Below: Location of aerial photograph shown on map 1 : 300 000

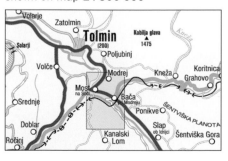

The Soča Valley affords the shortest route between the Alps and the Adriatic coast. Compared with other Slovene rivers the Soča is quite exceptional. Its length is a mere 140 km, yet its gradient is considerable: its source lies in Trenta, almost 900 m above sea level. The flow rate of the Soča is highly variable through the year. Heavy precipitation turns the river into a thunderous torrent which can wash away bridges. But the Soča is also famous for the uncommon aquamarine colour of its crystal clear water. The course of the Soča has to adapt to the boisterous geological history of the region. The river follows tectonic fault lines, cutting canyons whenever it encounters natural obstacles. Due to rock collapses and tectonic shifts, lakes have appeared and disappeared through the various geological periods. It is evident that the Soča Valley is geologically young and is still changing. The river features gorges and ravines and broad sand banks. Just before entering the Bovec plain, the Soča is only one metre wide, but only a short stretch downstream, at Čezsoča, it spills over the gravel deposits to a width of half a kilometre. At Solkan, where it crosses the frontier into Italy, the Soča takes leave of the mountains and meanders on the rest of its way to the Adriatic over the Friulian plain.

One would expect that the influence of the Mediterranean would reach along the Soča Valley far into the interior. In fact it stops already on the slopes of Sabotin. Some of the balmy warmth spills over to the Soča basin along the Valley of the Nadiža and the tributary of the Učja, and moderates the climate of the Kobarid and Bovec areas. The last signs of Mediterranean influence are the stands of Austrian pine in the valleys of the Koritnica and Trenta.

The Soča basin also includes two regions west of the Soča, Goriška Brda (Gorica Hills) and Breginjski kot (Breginj Pocket), although they belong to other geographical regions.

The fertile Brda Hills are the rolling hills sloping south towards the plain of Gorica and reaching the Friulian and Venetian hills on the other bank of the border river of Idrija. The post-war border demarcation almost completely

isolated Brda from the rest of Slovenia. The only link is provided by a road from the Soča Valley, which rises over a 300-m high pass at Vrhovlje. This obstacle was compensated for by the "Osimo" road which runs along the south-western slope of Sabotin and partly over Italian territory. The old fortified hilltop villages of Goriška Brda, where the houses crouch around narrow streets, and feudal castles lend authenticity to the landscape of several centuries ago, testify to a way of life which is slowly decaying only now. Thanks to their location on the fringes of the Friulian plain, the Brda hills have always been under strong cultural influences from northern and central Italy, which accounts for the "Renaissance" appearance of Brda's landscape. Telling examples of the building craft of bygone days are the village of Šmartno and Dobrovo manor. The second border region, Breginjski kot, which was for a brief time an autonomous "commune" under the Venetian Republic, was until recently a prime example of the sumptuous architecture of Venezia Giulia, featuring two-floor, stone-built houses, wooden balconies and baroque portals. The old part of Breginj, which suffered greatly in the 1976 earthquake, was never reconstructed.

Already in prehistoric times the Soča Valley provided the passage between the Friulian Plain and the valleys of the Alps. Since the valley did not afford easy passage throughout its length, points where the river could be safely forded played an important role. Early fortified settlements indicate the direction of the main transportation routes. A trail ran along the Soča Valley from Most na Soči to Kobarid, where it was joined by another trail from the Friulian plain which followed the Nadiža River. From Kobarid, the route continued along the canyon of the Soča to Bovec, and from there it wound along the Koritnica Valley and over the Predel Saddle to Carinthia. An important mercantile route led from Tolmin along the Bača Valley to Petrovo Brdo and Bohinj. Iron Age settlements were discovered on Ravelnik near Bovec, on the hill of St. Anton above Kobarid, and on Kozlov rob near Tolmin. One of the most famous archaeological sites is Most na Soči, formerly Sveta Lucija. About 6,000 early Iron Age graves (800–400 BC) have been excavated, and continuous settlement of the site has also been confirmed for the late Iron Age and Roman period. A settlement of log houses with stone foundations clearly indicates urbanisation tendencies in the early Iron Age.

Historians thought that with the fall of the Roman empire the Soča basin had lost its significance, but recent late-Antiquity finds at Tonovcov grad near Kobarid have proved them wrong. The proximity of Venice, and the Napoleonic wars in the 18th and 19th centuries, restored its strategic importance. The fortifications at Predel and Kluže indicate that the passage from Carinthia to the Soča Valley was at that time again an important strategic consideration. The Bohinj railway, built in 1906, brought modern transportation, linking the Sava Valley with the Gorica region, and introduced several remote regions to the rest of the world. Nevertheless, the upper reaches of the Soča Valley continued to be neglected in terms of transportation. The First World War produced enormous casualties on both sides of the Isonzo front. From 1915 to 1917, three hundred thousand soldiers from every corner of Europe lost their lives on the Isonzo battlefield, which stretched from the Kras to Rombon. When, in October 1917, the Italian front was penetrated at Kobarid, the bloodshed shifted from the Soča Valley to the Piave River. The end of the war in 1918 did not bring complete relief to the local population, because the national border cut off the Soča basin from the rest of Slovenia.

6 The abundant precipitation, mostly in the form of snow, which falls on the extensive Kaninski podi plateau, is not drained on the surface. Most of the water re-emerges from the karst spring in the rock face below Baba, and falls into the valley as the mighty, 106-m-high and 30-m-wide Boka waterfall. Most of the water flows into the Soča under the pebbles.

7 The Soča reaches Kobarid by a gorge between Stol and Polovnik to spread into the wide valley between Krn and Kolovrat.

8 A sad memorial of the First World War: the ossuary of fallen Italian soldiers around the church of St. Anton above Kobarid. The Kobarid Museum tells the story of the war in its exhibition.

9 Shrovetide is the time of the *psti*, masks from Drežnica below Krn.

10 The home at Vrsno, high above Soča Valley, where the poet Simon Gregorčič was born, has been turned into a museum.

11 The 15-m-high Veliki Kozjak waterfall is on the Kozjak stream, which rises below Krnčica.

12 The Idrijca valley (in the shadow), the Šentvid plateau, the Tolmin basin (the prominent hill is Kozlov rob), in the background the mountain ranges of Krn and Kanin.

11

12

39

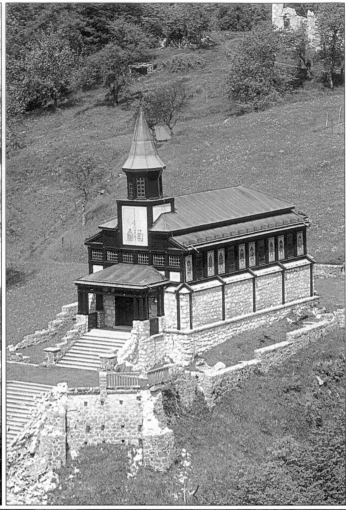

13 The lower course of the Tolminka cuts it way through narrow, up to 80-m-deep troughs and is joined by the Zadlaščica with its own troughs.

14 The church of the Holy Spirit was erected at Javorca above the Tolminka valley and the Polog alp in 1916, in memory of the fallen soldiers of the Austrian army on the Isonzo front.

15 Dobrovo is the centre of Goriška Brda. Its 17th-century mansion houses a museum collection, a gallery of prints by Zoran Mušič, and a concert hall.

16 Vedrijan and other villages amidst the vineyards of Goriška Brda, which produce *Zlata Rebula*, *Tokajec*, *Pinot*, *Karbernet*, and *Merlot*. The early fruit of the region, cherries and peaches, is at least as popular as the area's vine juices. The blossoming trees turn the sunny slopes into white tapestries earlier than anywhere else in Slovenia.

17 Nova Gorica is a modern town on the southern edge of the Gorica plain, founded by decree in 1947, when the border with Italy separated Gorizia/Gorica from its natural hinterland. The centre of the town delights with its rose beds, rare trees and bushes; over 30 public monuments are scattered over the town. A Franciscan monastery from the 17th century occupies the Kostanjevica hill, and the nearby Kromberk Castle houses the Gorica Museum. Over the past five decades strong links have been established with Gorizia/Gorica.

18 The Kostanjevica hill, dominating Nova Gorica, Rožna dolina and Gorizia/Gorica, is the site of a Franciscan monastery, which boasts a rich painting collection and a library. The presbitery of the church holds the tomb of the Bourbon royal family, with the sarcophagus of the last French king, Charles X Philippe.

16

17

18

The Northern Border

The Karavanke, Jezersko, the Meža Valley, the Mislinja Valley

1 The Karavanke extend around 120 km and are the longest mountain range in Slovenia. The Slovene-Austrian border runs along the highest ridges and summits; the road and railway connections with Central and West Europe are constructed across mountain passes and through tunnels.

Left: The southern slopes of Stol with the Završnica valley and the Radovljica plain at its foot
Below: Location of aerial photograph shown on map 1 : 300 000

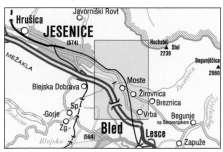

Karavanke, a name of proto-Indo-European origin, is reminiscent of Karantanija, the name of the first state of the Slovene nation and the Slavic nations in general, with its centre in present-day Carinthia, dating to the 8th century. The Karavanke chain is undoubtedly the greatest natural barrier within Slovene territory.

A rock wall of one hundred-and-twenty-kilometres between Trbiž and Slovenj Gradec, it separates the Slovenes of Carinthia from the Slovenes of Carniola and Styria. During the settlement of the Alps, migrations in some places spilled over the Karavanke to the south (the Upper Sava Valley as far as Gozd, Jezersko and the Upper Savinja Valley were settled from the Carinthian side). Later, the border following the ridge of the Karavanke also became a dividing line in the minds of the people on each side of the mountain range. In addition to other circumstances, this fact must have influenced the decision of Carinthian Slovenes to opt for Austria in the 1920 plebiscite. Today, the Karavanke coincide with the Slovene national border, and it is hoped that this natural barrier would present only an insignificant obstacle to both countries and the Slovenes on both sides.

In geological terms, the Karavanke differ from the Kamnik Alps, consisting mostly of late Paleozoic rock, from the Devonian onwards. Most of their mountain tops are composed of younger Mesozoic limestones and dolomites. In the past, scientists dwelled on the geological distinction of the Karavanke compared to the limestone composition of the neighbouring Alps. More recent theories on the existence of the so-called continental plates again put the Karavanke in the same group as the Kamnik Alps. According to the new theory, the Karavanke, the Julian Alps and their foothills belong to the large mountain-forming element of the Dinarides, while the Pohorje and regions of eastern Karavanke (Obir and Peca) belong to the Alpids. This interesting theory is also discussed below in 'Between the Paka and the Sotla Rivers').

The Karavanke feature many traces of volcanic activity. The last major volcanic activity was in the Tertiary period. Deposits of volcanic ash, agglomerated into green rock called tuff, date from this period. In Gorenjska, this volcanic rock was used as decorative material for window and door frames. The volcano itself was located in the vicinity of Smrekovec and Travnik, on the border between Štajerska and Koroška. The summit of Komen (1,684 m), for

2 The Dolžan gorge above Tržič is the most magnificent natural geological profile in Slovenia. A road and the Slovene Geological Path pass through the gorge.

3 Jezersko was the only pocket of the former Carinthia on the Sava side. The village can pride itself on some fine cultural monuments. Makek's granary is a fine example of vernacular architecture, and Jonko's "barracks" is an inn from the early 16ᵗʰ century.

4 Podolševa is a scattered area of isolated farms below Olševa (Karavanke) and Raduha (Savinja Alps), along the panoramic road which connects Solčava and Črna na Koroškem. An archaeological site on the slopes of Raduha dates from the period of the Pleistocene hunters (35,000 to 22,000 BC).

5 Bukovnik, the highest located homestead in Slovenia (1,327 m); in the background the Savinja Alps and the Karavanke.

6 Boundary stones in the Kokra valley, marking the onetime border between the provinces of Carniola and Carinthia.

example, is composed of volcanic andezite. Several rare plants have established their habitat on this (unusual in Slovenia) rock, e.g. the *primula villosa* and *campanula alpina*.

The entire geological history of the Karavanke can be viewed in the short, yet picturesque Dolžan Gorge near Tržič. The Tržiška Bistrica has cut across the rock layers and exposed several rock types deposited over a long period which began with the mid-Paleozoic and ended with the Triassic. Some of the strata contain fascinating rocks, many of which were first identified at this site.

In terms of altitude, the Karavanke are no match for the neighbouring Julian Alps to the south. Only the highest peak, Mt. Stol (2,236 m), reaches above the 2,200-m level. But the panoramas of the Sava and the Drava basins from the Karavanke viewpoints are as magnificent as any. The southern slopes of the Karavanke are markedly different from their northern slopes. The familiar peaks are unrecognizable from the other side. The southern side is easily negotiable and covered with grass; the northern side has almost nothing but precipitous rock faces. A maverick of the Karavanke peaks is Košuta, a 10-km long ridge with 2,000-m high peaks and a mighty north face. At the foot of the Ljubelj slope, Tržič emerged in the Middle Ages. The original settlement was buried by a landslide and present-day Tržič (first mentioned in 1320) was built lower in the valley. Market town since 1492.

Two pockets of Carinthia remained within the borders of Slovenia: the smaller of the two is Jezersko, the larger is the Meža Valley. In the latter traditional industry has survived to the present day. At Prevalje, there was an ironworks in the 19ᵗʰ century, and now the town of Ravne continues this tradition. The Meža Valley was serviced by a railway line quite early on, which, in 1863, connected Maribor and Klagenfurt (Celovec) by way of the low-lying pass of Holmec. Holmec, more accurately nearby Poljana, is the site of the last European battle in the Second World War. The remnants of the retreating German forces and those of the Independent State of Croatia and Montenegrin Chetniks tried to fight their way to Austria, but were defeated by the Yugoslav Army.

The upper part of the Meža Valley, populated by the mining towns of Mežica, Žerjav and Črna, branches out into two picturesque valleys: the Topla, with five large solitary farms at the foot of Peca, and Koprivna at the foot of Olševa, with more solitary farms and a parish church. Favourable nature conditions made the highest permanent settlement possible in Slovenia precisely in this region. Particularly of note are the homesteads of Jekl (1,322 m) in Koprivna, and Bukovnik (1,327 m) on Sleme above Solčava.

Olševa (1,929 m) is a ridge-shaped mountain which achieved international fame thanks to the 1928 discovery of an Early Stone Age settlement in the karst cave of Potočka zijalka. About thirty-five thousand years ago, an Ice Age hunting camp stood at this site.

To the east, the northern chain of the Karavanke ends in the imposing mountains of Peca (2,125 m) and somewhat humbler Uršlja gora (1,699 m). Peca's enormous mass of limestone with a flattened summit is traversed by the national border, with the larger half on the Austrian side. And according to legend, *Kralj Matjaž* (King Matthew) and his army are still sleeping in the bosom of the mountain.

▶

7

8

9

10

11

46

7 The Topla valley is a pearl in the Koroška landscape. Five isolated farms nestle on the sunny slopes below Peca. The valley was protected as a landscape park in 1966.

8 Koroška has rich cultural monuments. Two old Gothic churches stand above Leše on Volinjek: St. Anne (foreground), and St. Volbenk (background, deprived of its tower, which lightning destroyed in 1885). The old linden tree next to the church has a circumference of 445 cm. Koroška is known for its numerous old trees.

9 Ravne na Koroškem, a modern industrial and ironworks centre, is the biggest urban settlement in the Meža valley. The town is dotted with Forma Viva iron sculptures (and there are some more in Prevalje, Kotlje, and Črna na Koroškem).

10 The memorial to the writer Lovro Kuhar – Prežihov Voranc stands on Preški Vrh, where he lived for some time.

11 Strojna is a mountain settlement of isolated farms, scattered on the sunny slopes of the mountain of the same name. Some of the homesteads are fine examples of vernacular architecture from the 17th and 18th centuries.

12 Libeliče, a village above the Drava in Koroška, refused to have its destiny decided from outside. When it was allocated to Austria after the 1920 plebiscite, the villagers were adamant in their request to be incorporated into Slovenia, and they achieved that the border was moved to the other side of the village in 1922. A famous round Roman ossuary, one of the few preserved in Slovenia, stands at the church.

13 Slovenj Gradec is the economic and administrative centre of the Mislinja Valley and the cultural heart of Koroška. The town has a modern hospital, the Koroška Regional Museum and the Soklič Museum, the Gallery of the Fine Arts, and, from the older heritage, the parish church, consecrated to St. Elizabeth in 1251, and a church of the Holy Spirit from the early 15th century. The church of St. Pancratius on the Castle Hill (Grajski grič) is a rebuilt 13th-century castle.

12

13

The Alps with Two Names

The Kamnik and Savinja Alps, Kamnik, the Upper Savinja Valley

1 The 9-km-long glacier-shaped Logar Valley, the biggest in the Savinja Alps (a landscape park), and the village of Logarska Dolina. Here the Savinja rises and the environs feature several other natural and cultural sights.

Left: The Kamnik Saddle, joining the Kamnik (left) and the Logar flanks (right)
Below: Location of aerial photograph shown on map 1 : 300 000

Of the three ranges of the southern limestone Alps in Slovenia, i.e., the Julian Alps, the Karavanke, and the Kamnik and Savinja Alps (Kamniško-Savinjske Alpe), the last is the smallest, but has the longest name. Before the foundation of the state of SHS (Serbs, Croatians and Slovenes) in 1918, this highland region was divided between the three provinces of Carinthia, Styria and Carniola. The triple border point was at Križ (2,429 m), which is evidenced by the names of nearby peaks: Koroška Rinka (which is another name for Križ), Štajerska Rinka, and Kranjska Rinka.

It has been often observed that the Grintovci (the old name for the loftiest cluster of peaks from Kočna, and the highest, 2,558 m Grintovec, to Ojstrica) are a smaller version of the Julian Alps. The entire massif is a star-shaped mountain range with short, yet scenic valleys. The headwaters of the Sava tributaries, the Kokra, the Kamniška Bistrica, and the Savinja lie in this region, while the Bela flows into the Drava.

The Ice Age, which ended about ten thousand years ago, did not have a major impact on this narrow and steep group of peaks as the glaciers were rather short. There are two glacial valleys on the Kokra side called Ravenska Kočna and Makekova Kočna, and of the three parallel valleys on the Savinja side the centrally situated Logar Valley (Logarska dolina) is a textbook example of a glacial valley.

The Savinja side has an interesting history of nature conservation. The Igla (The Needle), a 40-metre high rock tower in the gorge between Luče and Solčava, and a nearby intermittent source attracted the attention of scientists in the 19th century. The Igla and the old yew tree of Solčava have been protected as natural monuments since 1951. The majestic beauty of the Logar Valley charmed its earliest visitors, and between the two wars, Celje mountaineers suggested protecting it. In 1931, 426 hectares of the land around Okrešelj were purchased for this purpose as an initial step towards a national park. Today, this idea is coming true in the form of the emerging regional nature reserve.

On the Kamnik side of the Alps, traces of an early Bronze Age settlement have been discovered high in the mountains. The archaic craft of building herdsmen's cottages on the Velika planina plateau may be the legacy of ancient shepherds. The lowest-lying passage from the town of Kamnik to the Savinja

2 The stream which rises under the Okrešelj cirque forms the 90-m-high Rinka waterfall. It is one of highest free-falling waterfalls in Slovenia. The water's fall is broken by a tufa cone at the bottom, disappears in the rubble and resurfaces in the middle of the Logar Valley as the Črna river. At its confluence with the Jezera, which rises in the Matkov kot valley, it becomes the Savinja.

3 Robanov kot, a picturesque Alpine valley with several isolated farms and an area of 1880 ha, has been under special protection since 1950. The Bela torrent washes down dolomite rubble from the slopes of Ojstrica (background) and Krofička (right), which close off the southern side of the valley.

4 This 40-m-high solitary rock, the Igla (Needle), stands in a gorge near the Luče-Solčava road. Under it is a periodic spring.

5 The river, Alpine valley, and scattered village which share the name Kamniška Bistrica are on the southern side of the Kamnik Alps. The river flows through two troughs and there are several interesting subterranean caves in the slopes.

6 The Savinja has preserved its natural appearance in its upper course and down to Ljubno ob Savinji.

7 Gornji Grad is a settlement in the upper part of the Dreta valley, on the road which leads from the Ljubljana basin across the Črnivec pass into the Upper Savinja Valley. The church of St. Hermagora and St. Fortunatus was in former times a residence of the bishops of Ljubljana. It counts as the most spacious church in Slovenia.

8 Kamnik is located on the margin of the Kamnik plain, at the foot of the Kamnik Alps. The small medieval town, which has partially preserved its historical core, developed on the once main trade route between the Danube basin and the Adriatic Sea. Today it is an administrative, economic, and cultural centre. The ruins of Mali grad (Little Castle) occupy a rock promontory in the middle of the town; they consist of remains of defence walls, a rectangular tower, and two chapels (the bottom one dates from around 1100, the top one from the 13th century); the ruins are a monument of the development of architecture of European significance.

Valley, via the Tuhinj Valley was, on the Carniolan side, controlled by Kamnik, a community mentioned for the first time in the mid-12th century, which received a town charter around 1220. Another old route, closer to the Alps, ran over the 902 metre high Črnivec pass. On the other side of the pass, at the headwaters of the Dreta, the old settlement of Gornji Grad emerged. In 1140 a Benedictine monastery was founded here, which later became the summer residence of the Ljubljana bishops. The third old borough at the foot of the Alps which controlled the passage from the Upper Savinja Valley towards the Celje basin and the Šalek Valley was Mozirje. The first mention of the community dates from the 12th century. Timber was rafted from Ljubno, past Mozirje down the Savinja, and further downstream to buyers on the Sava. From the summer of 1944 to the end of the same year, Solčava and a large part of the Upper Savinja Valley were declared liberated partisan territory bordering on the Third Reich.

Hills, Forests and Plains

The Pohorje, the Drava Valley, Kozjak, Košenjak

1 The Pohorje is a 50-km-long mountain range, largely covered by conifer forests, in the north-east of Slovenia, bordered to the north by the Drava, and to the south and east by the Mislinja valley, the Vitanje network of valleys, the Dravinja hills and the Drava and Ptuj plains. The Pohorje has abundant natural (peat bogs, giant trees) and cultural sights (solitary farms, vernacular architecture, churches).

Left: The Vuhred hydroelectric station on the river Drava
Below: Location of aerial photograph shown on map 1 : 300 000

On the right bank of the Drava there rises the 50-km long dome-like Pohorje mountain range. The main ridge spans the distance between Dravograd and Maribor in a gently curving arch. In the highest and also the widest central section, the ridge branches out towards the south, but only so far as to form a thick central area, giving the entire mountain range the shape of a crescent.

The Pohorje is the only part of the Slovenian Alps which in fact belongs to the Central Alpine chain, though it is considerably lower. The highest peaks, due to their rounded tops, hardly deserve that name, barely clearing the 1500-metre mark: Črni vrh (1,543 m), Velika Kopa (1,542 m), Jezerski vrh (1,537 m), Muljev vrh (1,533 m), and the centrally located Rogla (1,517 m). Moderate elevation, however, is all that we can hold against the Pohorje. This shortcoming is compensated for by several other features found nowhere else in Slovenia. Only on the the Pohorje can we truly grasp the vastness of the mountains. Here we are not troubled by the claustrophobia or vertigo. There is no off-season for the Pohorje meadows, which are ideal for winter trekking as well as summer hikes. Here, the wilderness can be enjoyed at any time of the year and in any weather conditions. The principal natural resource of the Pohorje is the forest. More than a hundred years ago, there was the sound of the lumberjack's axe, the smoke of charcoal making, and chutes for skidding lumber to the saw mills, forges and glassworks. Due to clear-cut logging, many mountainsides were exposed to the elements, but eventually overgrown by raspberry bushes and *Chamaeneroin angustifolium*. Now, this is only a memory, while Pohorje continues to live a very different existence.

From the plateau-like top of the Pohorje, many streams flow in all directions. Some of them eventually become true rivers: the Mislinja, the Radoljna, the Lobnica, the Polskava, the Bistrica, the Dravinja. All of them flow into the Drava, except the Hudinja and the Paka, which swing due south and join the Savinja. The swiftest river flowing into the Drava is the abundant Lobnica, with the lake of Črno jezero as its source. Its course also features two waterfalls, Veliki Šumik and Mali Šumik. On the steep mountainsides above the Lobnica gulley, the last patch of the Pohorje's virgin forest has been preserved, spared the axe by the sheer steepness of the terrain.

2

3

5

4

2 The Radlje plain along the Drava is around 6 km long and 2 km wide. Here are the Vuzenica in Vuhred power plants on the Drava. In Radlje ob Dravi a turn-off leads across the Radlje international border crossing into the Graz basin.

3 The church of St. John the Baptist, a basically Romanesque rotunda, supposed to have been consecrated in the mid 11th century, stands on a little hill at the confluence of the Bistrica stream and the Drava near Spodnja Muta

4 The Pohorje in its winter outfit is an attractive destination for skiers. The main skiing centres are near Maribor, on Rogla above Zreče, and on Kope above Slovenj Gradec.

5 Šentjanž nad Dravčami is a Pohorje settlement of isolated farms above the Drava. Some homesteads have preserved their original appearance; a mighty Scotch pine grows at the Dravčbaher homestead. The church of St. John the Baptist from the 15th century stands on a promontory above the village.

6 This monument near Osankarica on the Pohorje stands at the site of the last stand of the Partisan Pohorje Battalion, which was completely wiped out in a clash with overwhelmingly superior German forces on January 8, 1943.

Peat bogs developed in several places along the entire ridge between Rogla and the peak of Jezerski vrh. These are singular wetland areas fed by rainwater, most often occurring precisely at the top of the ridge, on Planinka, for example. A marshland, with a small lake called Ribniško jezerce, bounded by dwarf pine, lies below the peak of Jezerski vrh.

The rock composition of the Pohorje is quite unusual for Slovenia. The major part of the mountain mass is composed of various metamorphic rocks of the Paleozoic era. Among these recrystallized rocks, a small deposit of true white marble has been discovered near Slovenska Bistrica, which was quarried during the Roman period. The core of the Pohorje is composed of a vast layer of 'tonalit' (nowadays granodiorit, erroneously called granite). Tonalit is formed from magma which is extruded from the earth's core to just below the surface and gradually cooled there. Similar to tonalit is čizlakit, a rare greenish granular rock, which has been found at Cezlak and is a rarity in Slovenia. This rock has the distinction of adorning the facade of the National Assembly Building. The third rock type found on the Pohorje is dacit, making up the western part of the ridge. Dacit also originates from magma which penetrates the earth's surface, where it cools and hardens.

At the western foot of the Pohorje lies Slovenj Gradec, an old town of rich cultural tradition. The name of the town speaks of the early settlement of the Slovenians around 800 AD. The oldest part of the town is called Stari trg, the successor to a Roman settlement.

The southern fringe of the Pohorje reaches as far as Vitanjsko podolje (the Vitanje Valley). It lies along a fault line running from Lavanttal in Austria along the Drava to Dravograd; it continues along the Mislinja Valley (Mislinjska dolina), crosses the Paka, passes through Vitanje and Stranice, and ends near Slovenjske Konjice at the Dravinja. This low-altitude passage from Štajerska to Koroška was used already in the Roman period and in the Middle Ages, but lost its importance when a passage was opened along the narrow Drava Valley between the Pohorje and Kozjak. At major crossroads, two old boroughs of Radlje and Dravograd developed. Decades ago, Dravograd was Slovenia's leading railway intersection for lines to Štajerska and Koroška. The high-altitude region north of the Drava has poor transportation facilities and so is less known. Košenjak (1,522 m) towers above Dravograd, echoing the Pohorje in terms of elevation and rock composition. It is in fact the southernmost extremity of Golica (Koralpe), a mountain range on the other side of the border, separated from the neighbouring wide-stretched Kozjak by the deep valley of the Mučka Bistrica. The slopes of Kozjak are lower than those of Košenjak, cut through by numerous gullies and ravines. Along one such valley runs the old road to the present-day international border crossing at Radlje.

At the end of the Drava gorge, on the outskirts of Maribor, an unusually large river island has formed a short distance downstream from the rapids. Today, the island (Mariborski otok) is practically a nature reserve and has been protected as a natural sight since 1951.

7 A large peat bog, called the Lovrenc bog (Lovrenško barje, Lovrenška jezera) lies on the Planinka ridge in the central section of the Pohorje, on the watershed between the Radoljna, Mislinja and Velka rivers. The bog has the greatest variety of plant species of all the Pohorje bogs.

8 The northern slopes of the Pohorje are forested and shady, but the southern ones show a quite different appearance. The sunny slopes are settled, and at the foot eminent Pohorje wines are grown, among them the famous Ritoznojčan.

9 In Skomarje, a scattered settlement on the southern slopes of the Rogla section of the Pohorje, a typical Skomarje house has been preserved and turned into a museum. The building is a representative example of the transitional type between a *dimnica* (subalpine elongated, shingle-covered, chimneyless wooden cabin) and a house with the "black kitchen".

10 The Veliki Šumik waterfall in the Lobnica gorge flows down a rock step over a length of 36 m. Further below is the Mali Šumik waterfall. The two are the biggest and most scenic falls on the Pohorje.

11 Slovenska Bistrica is the biggest settlement at the southern foot of the Pohorje. The settlement, called *Pultovia* in the Roman era, developed at the junction of the roads which connect Celje, Maribor, and Ptuj; in the 13th century it was a market-place and it became a town between 1297 and 1310. The castle in the middle of the town was first mentioned in the 13th century, and was Baroque rebuilt in the 17th century. Its biggest room is the Knights' Hall which is decorated with wall paintings.

12 The Dolar (or Robič) chestnut tree is a famous sight on the Hoče Pohorje. With its circumference of 830 cm, it is one of the biggest chestnut trees in Slovenia.

13 The church of sv. Areh (St. Henry) is the principal cultural monument of the eastern Pohorje. It was first mentioned in 1545.

The Drava Plain

Maribor, the Drava Plain, the Ptuj Plain, Haloze

1 Maribor is the second biggest town of Slovenia in terms of area, population, and economic importance; it is also the cultural, education, and health care capital of north-east Slovenia. The town is located on the border between the Alps and the Pannonian Plain.

Most of the north-eastern part of Slovenia hinges on the River Drava. The waters of the Drava flow from the snowfields of Carinthia and Tyrol and enter Slovenia as a full-fledged river. The highest annual water flow is reached at the beginning of summer, when most Slovene rivers are at their lowest flow rate. Since time immemorial the Drava has been an important watercourse, especially for rafts. Today, it is difficult to imagine that people once panned for gold on the banks of the Drava. Numerous dams in Austria and Slovenia prevented gold-bearing sediments, which were quite poor in gold content in the first place, from being carried downriver.

A stretch of 142 km of the Drava, from Dravograd to Središče, flows through Slovenia. From here, Slovenia shares the river for some distance with neighbouring Croatia. Since 1918, when the first hydroelectric plant, Fala, began operating, a total of eight such power plants have been built. All the electric energy potential of the river has been harnessed, but the lively murmur of the river is gone forever.

Downstream from Maribor, beyond the outcrops of the Pohorje and Kozjak ranges, there is room for the plain of Dravsko polje. This is a triangular plain covered with alluvial deposits and fringed by the foothills of Pohorje, Haloze and Slovenske gorice. The streams from the south-eastern edge of Pohorje covered the dry gravel sediments with a layer of clay, thus extending their courses.

Several low-lying areas turned into marshland, and where the land was not suitable for farming it was overgrown by flood-plain forest (the vicinity of Pragersko, and Cigonca near Slovenska Bistrica). To prevent the flooding of fields, streams were diverted to the marshes, straightened and lined by embankments. Due to the continuous deposition of alluvial gravel, regular dredging of the river beds and rebuilding of the embankments, the streams eventually rose above the level of the surrounding fields. The banks became overgrown with vegetation and shrubbery, creating a picturesque effect of green lines crisscrossing the landscape.

At Ptuj, the Dravsko polje becomes Ptujsko polje. This is a fertile plain dotted with friendly villages, the home of carnival masks called *kurenti*, and other rural traditions.

Left: The Drava Plain with the village of Pleterje
Below: Location of aerial photograph shown on map 1 : 300 000

2

3

4

5

2 The efforts of the guardians of the town's cultural heritage are aimed at renovating Maribor's river port (Lent) on the left bank of the Drava. The photograph captures the entire historical core of the town.

3 The *Žametovka* vine at Lent is at least 300 years old and continues to bear fruit.

4 The preserved Water Tower shows some typical Renaissance style characteristics; the renovated Jewish Tower stands in the background and is incorporated into the town walls. The initially unwanted reservoir now blends with the new appearance of the town.

5 Glavni trg, the Main Square, is Maribor's market centre. Its renovation, including the Town Hall and the Plague Column, a reminder of the medieval scourge, restored the square's original splendour.

6 Straub's statue from the church of St. Joseph in Studenci is on view in the Maribor Regional Museum.

7 Remains of the natural riverbed, here at Malečnik, is all that is left of the old course of the Drava.

South of the Dravinja, the largest right-hand tributary of the Drava in Slovenia, the plain begins to rise to meet the rolling hills of Haloze. The hills and dales are of soft rock, mostly Tertiary marl. The typical Haloze landscape features gently sloping fields, vineyards on steeper, sunny slopes, forest-covered northern slopes and marshes in the valleys. A bird's-eye-view from the nearby mountain reveals the patchwork of this dynamic district.

Beyond the hills of Haloze, a crescent of limestone mountains rises sharply. From east to west there follow the mountains of Macelj (718 m), Donačka gora (882 m) and Boč, the highest among them (only 20 metres short of the one thousand mark), whose dark peak dominates much of Štajerska. And yet only Donačka (or Rogaška) gora deserves to be called a mountain. Despite its average elevation, it boasts every other attribute of a true mountain: rock walls, a sharp ridge and a characteristic silhouette, easily recognizable from afar. From the side, as seen from Rogaška Slatina or Žetale, it appears as a conical horn, and from the Dravsko polje, it has the form of a table. And yet the mountain has an even greater significance. Its northern slope hides a large stand of virgin beech forest, while the peak ridge and the sunny rocks harbour rare plant and animal life such as *Sempervivum juvanii*, indigenous to this area.

The region by the Drava was settled quite early. The Romans reached the river during the reign of their first emperor, Augustus, in the last few decades BC. In the Ptuj area, an army outpost of the Roman legion was set up. When the legion was transferred in the winter of 14 to 15 AD to the Danubian frontier, the military fort became a civilian settlement. The Roman town of Poetovio was granted municipal rights at the end of the 1st century and was the largest Roman township in the territory of present-day Slovenia. The town was famous for its large stone bridge and a road which led to the Pannonian Plain.

8 Betnava Mansion on the edge of the town is a fine example of Late Baroque representative architecture from the 18th century. After decades of negligence and inadequate use the mansion is now given an appearance that befits its value as a monument.

9 The Orpheus Memorial in Ptuj, situated by the Town Tower in the Slovenski trg square. It was erected to commemorate Marcus Valerius Verus lord, mayor in the 2nd century AD. It counts as the oldest ornamented public monument in Slovenia, standing on the very spot where it was set up.

10 Some of the exquisite halls of Ptuj Castle are decorated with furnishings from the feudal era.

11 Below Ptuj, a nearly 2000-year-old town, the fast flowing Drava was stopped by another reservoir. The town and its environs are dominated by a medieval castle which houses the Regional Museum.

12 Ptuj with its surroundings is characterised by a number of temples dedicated to the West-Asiatic god Mithras. The statue showing Mithras shouldering a bull, from 150 or 160 AD, is displayed in a Mithraeum, rearranged as an open-air museum, at Spodnja Hajdina.

Among the many special features of the architecture of ancient Ptuj, three temples consecrated to the Oriental god Mithras deserve mention. Roman Ptuj was supplied with drinking water by a water supply system of aqueducts from Pohorje. The ruins of the system, found between Fram and Ptuj, testify to the entrepreneurial spirit of the ancient inhabitants of Ptuj.

In the Middle Ages, too, traffic centered around the Drava, particularly at river-crossing sites. Ptuj preserved its ancient role as a crossing point. A new settlement emerged upstream, where the Drava emerges from a narrow valley. The site is first mentioned in 1209 as a trading center, and soon afterward, in 1254, as a town, named civitas Marpurg. This German name was used until the rise of Slovene nationalism when, in 1836, the town was renamed Maribor. The new, resonant name took root also because the town's Slovene population increased and Maribor became the center of Slovene Styria, counterbalancing the German-speaking city of Graz.

Maribor and Ptuj competed in crafts and commerce through the Middle Ages and well into modern times, until the arrival of the southern railway line, which reached Maribor in 1846. Because of the lack of foresight of the contemporary municipal administration, the railway bypassed Ptuj and took the shortest route to the coast. From that time, Ptuj remained in Maribor's shadow, and somewhat recovered from oblivion with the advent of the railway in 1861 connecting Pragersko with Velika Kaniža in Hungary via Ptuj. Thus developed the first railway crossroads in Slovenia at Pragersko, an intersection of the three main routes of the Habsburg monarchy linking Vienna, Budapest and Trieste.

Ormož was the river-crossing point on the Drava nearest to Croatia which then belonged to Hungary. Ormož is an old town which acquired municipal rights in the Middle Ages, when the fortified castle high above the Drava oversaw all river traffic. Reminders of the time when border skirmishes between the Hungarians and the Turks were frequent are also to be found in the nearby castle of Velika Nedelja, the seat of the German Knights of the Cross. Around the fortified castles grew boroughs and towns such as Slovenska Bistrica and Slovenske Konjice.

The Drava region features two exceptional monuments of medieval architecture. The first is the former Carthusian monastery of Žiče, founded in 1164 and dissolved in 1782, located in a remote valley at the foot of Konjiška gora. The ruins of the Gothic church and a part of the former monastery, representative of European Carthusian architecture, still survive. The second example is the Old-Slavonic pilgrimage church on Ptujska gora, which was built at the end of the 14th century by the counts of Celje and Ptuj, and is estimated as the most perfect example of three-nave Gothic hall-like church in Slovenia. Overlooking the Dravinja Valley stands the 18th-century baroque mansion of Štatenberg with its magnificent frescoes.

Following World War I, the Drava region was granted to Slovenia, as part of the new Kingdom of the Serbs, Croats and Slovenes, for two reasons. The first was the taking of Maribor by General Rudolf Maister and his Slovene army in November 1918. Then, according to the Peace Treaty of Trianon, in the summer of 1919, the region of Prekmurje and the mining region of the Mežica Valley (also because of the vested interests of foreign capital) were also granted to Slovenia.

▶

13

15

14

16

13 Ancient customs have been preserved on the Ptuj plain, where magic creatures chase away winter and herald spring. Among the best-known masks are the enigmatically decorated Kurents.

14 Velika Nedelja prides itself on two architectural monuments: an initially Romanesque church, later enlarged, and the mighty castle of a former member of the German Order of the Knights of the Cross.

15 In the late 14th and early 15th centuries this monument of Gothic art, architecture and furnishings was created in the Dravinja hills – the Pilgrimage Church on Ptujska Gora.

16 The hills of Haloze consist of soft marl and quartz sandstone – sediments of the Pannonian sea in the Miocene. Numerous streamlets turned them into a hill range with a varied relief. There are few places where the landscape is as varied and the people as open-hearted as in Haloze.

17 The big Baroque Dornava Mansion on the Ptuj plain was erected by count Dizma Attems in the 18th century.

18 Štatenberg is a representative Baroque mansion, erected between 1720 and 1740. The entire varied complex of buildings, including their interior furnishings and wall paintings, radiates the spirit of the period. It is one of the most authentically preserved Baroque mansions in Slovenia.

17

18

From Goričko to Gorice

Goričko, Ravensko, Dolinsko, the Slovenske gorice

1 Grad is an extensive complex of castle buildings which has no match anywhere near. It stands in the east of Goričko, on a hill made up of basalt tufa and volcanic ash layers from the Pliocene. In its present condition, it is but a shadow of its former glory when it was occupied by Knights Templars. The castle is under renovation and is surrounded by a big park with old trees.

Left: The Veliki Brebovnik wine-growing area, part of Ljutomer-Ormož vineyards
Below: Location of aerial photograph shown on map 1 : 300 000

In Slovenia, the first rays of morning sun touch Lendavske gorice 13 minutes before they reach the peak of Muzec in the Kobariški Stol range, 240 kilometres away, at the westernmost tip of Slovenia. The easternmost corner of Slovenia lies a few kilometres more to the east, at the confluence of the Ledava and the Krka of Prekmurje, near the point where they both flow into the Mura. And yet, this is not the only geographical extremity of Prekmurje. The northernmost point of Slovenia lies at Goričko, near the village of Budinci, at latitude 46° 53'.

Goričko is the northernmost region of Slovenia. The name Goričko refers to a hilly region between the Mura and the Raba, an area which for over a thousand years has been the meeting point of three peoples: Slovene, German and Hungarian. Here also is the meeting point of the state borders of Hungary, Austria and Slovenia. However, the official borders do not follow the national borders. After 1919, when the present eastern border was determined, several Slovenian villages in the Porabje region remained in Hungary, while Lendava and several villages with a predominantly Hungarian population were embraced by the Yugoslav border.

The Mura, a large river of the Eastern Alps, changes its character in Slovenia. The swift watercourse turns into a sluggish river, with a wide, gravel-lined river bed and willow trees. The river is a historical dividing line between Slovenes in Austria and Slovenes in Hungary. Until the end of World War I, Prekmurje belonged to the Hungarian half of the Austro-Hungarian Empire, and only the Venetian Slovenes (in the extreme west, in Italy) were more isolated from their homeland, following the plebiscite in 1866. The inclusion of Prekmurje in Slovenia also meant a readjustment of the traditional administrative centres and main thoroughfares. Until the creation of the Kingdom of the Serbs, Croats and Slovenes, Murska Sobota was only a trading settlement in the centre of Ravensko, subsisting in the shade of the old boroughs of Dolnja Lendava and Gornja Lendava (which was the name of the near-forgotten Grad in Goričko). Sobota gained prominence with the advent of the railway, which in 1907 connected it via Šalovci with Hungary. Decisive for its development was the new state border, which placed Sobota at the centre of

2 Several storage ponds have been created in the valleys of Prekmurje's streams and rivers in the past decades. Water birds (here a grey heron) search Ledava Lake for food.

3 Goričko is a hilly landscape, consisting of soft sediments (clay, sand, rubble); it covers more than half the Slovene territory between the Austrian and Hungarian borders. Pine and mixed forests prevail, while the agricultural areas are worked with great care.

4 The chapel of St. Nicholas, probably from the 13th century, stands in the valley of the Kobiljanski potok stream at the edge of the village of Selo. There are two layers of frescoes in the interior, one from the first third of the 14th century, and a second one from the early 15th century.

5 Many old crafts (blacksmiths, wheelwrights) have almost become extinct, others will probably survive as they have found new customers. The attractive products of Prekmurje potters are still known all over Slovenia as decorative objects or souvenirs.

6 The church of the Ascension in Bogojina is a masterpiece designed by architect Jože Plečnik.

Prekmurje. Until then, Prekmurje had no traffic connections with the Styrian region. Until the construction of the road bridge at Veržej in 1922 and the advent of the railway from Ormož via Ljutomer to Murska Sobota in 1924 there were no bridges over the Mura. The traffic was left to ferrymen. Until a few years ago the ferry and the floating mill were typical features of the Mura. Owing to its isolation from other Slovene regions, Prekmurje has preserved a number of original features, dialect, music and folklore.

Individual finds of stone implements (axes, ploughs and hoes) from the Late Stone Age testify to the early settlement of Pomurje. There are few finds from the prehistoric period. Recently, archaeological discoveries at Šafarsko village have completely changed our view of the Late Stone Age settlement of the region. The excavated remains of the villages have revealed ancient agriculture.

The Roman presence in the area is seen in several sepulchral mounds and the remains of a settlement near Lendava beside the former Roman road leading from Poetovio (Ptuj) past Lendava to Savario (Szombathely). Except for the ancient Slovene settlement at Veržej in the 10th century, there were no other finds from the early period of Slovene settlement.

At the site of present-day Lendava, a settlement called Lindau sprang up in the Frankish period. In the 9th century, at the time of Pribina and Kocelj, Lindau was part of Slovene territory and was later transferred to Hungarian rule. The seat of the feudal property was Landava Castle, around which developed the town of Lendava, which in 1366 obtained market rights. The town suffered greatly under Turkish forays into the area, but developed faster after 1867, when it became a regional center. In 1890 the railway line from Čakovec connected it to other towns in Hungary.

Another old settlement is Grad (formerly Gornja Lendava), which developed beneath a majestic 12th century castle. The castle is among the biggest in Slovenia, now acquiring a new image under thorough renovation; there is also an extensive park with numerous big trees. Being now restored it gradually assumes the role of the centre of the Goričko regional park.

A famous place of more recent vintage is Velika Polana, the birthplace of Miško Kranjec, a prolific Slovene writer who described the youth of Prekmurje and the hard, yet idyllic, traditional village life.

On the south bank of the Mura, on a tributary called Ščavnica, lies the old market town of Ljutomer, which entered national history as the site of the first Slovene nationalist demonstration, *tabor*, on 9 August 1868. Of course, Ljutomer is also the center of Prlekija, the more common name for Mursko polje, the wine-producing district of Ljutomer-Ormož hills, where grape varieties such as Laški Riesling, Šipon, Traminer and Sauvignon, known throughout Europe, are grown. To the north-east, the Slovenske gorice hills spill over the state border and into Austrian Styria. The center of the Slovenske gorice is the old market town of Lenart above Pesnica. Lenart is connected by road to Maribor, which also runs to Gornja Radgona, the northernmost municipality in Slovenia. The town first grew beneath a castle which dominated the ancient passage over the Mura, with its counterpart called Bad Radkersburg lying on the other side of the river. Radgona entered Slovene history with the mutiny of Slovene soldiers in the Austro-Hungarian army in May 1918. There were also a few victims here during the war of independence in 1991. The hinterland, Radgonsko-Kapelske gorice (Radgona-Kapela hills) is again a well-known wine-producing area with a popular local wine variety called Janževec, and a sparkling wine, Zlata penina.

At the foot of the Kapelske gorice the health spa of Radenci developed around famed mineral water springs. The first spring was discovered in 1834. The spa became known after 1882 and is still being developed.

7 Prekmurje's subterranean riches are hot and mineral springs along the tectonic fault. Some springs are natural, others are the result of drilling for oil. Among the latter are Moravske Toplice, established in 1960, where the water temperature reaches 65 °C.

8 The development of the landscape along the Mura is changing life. Old villages are losing their traditional appearance, and peasant houses, like this one in Ravensko, will gradually disappear, while a handful will be preserved as museum specimens.

9 The Ravensko plain has a truly Pannonian appearance: wheat, maize, rye, and sugar beet thrive on the fertile soil.

10 Lendava, also called Lendva in Hungarian, is the seat of a bilingual municipality, in which for over a thousand years two nations, Slovenes and Hungarians, have lived together. The easternmost town in Slovenia, located at the foot of the Lendava hills, has vigorously revived and strengthened its links with Hungary.

11 The trademark of the vineyard hills is the wind rattle; they are all alike, but even in one place you won't find a pair of equal ones. This one is from the environs of Jeruzalem.

12 Murska Sobota, the centre of Prekmurje, continues to develop. The oldest part of the town is the castle with its extensive park.

Among the cultural monuments of Slovenia there is an unusual circular brick chapel dedicated to St. Nicholas, near the village of Selo in Prekmurje. The Romanesque-style building, known as the Rotunda, was built in the 13th century. The interior is famous for its 14th and 15th century Gothic frescoes.

A few traces of primaeval plant and animal life help us to envisage the watery wilderness of the Pannonian fringes. Thus near Petanjci, Hotiza and Petišovci, many ox-bow lakes (abandoned meanders, called *mrtvice*) can be found. They were cut off from the running water of the river and are now lined by dense vegetation, reeds, and bushes. In this calm water, plants can be found which are either very rare in Slovenia or found nowhere else (such as the water fern *Salvinia natans* and *Stratiotes aloides*). Recently, zoologists have discovered many animal species in these ox-bow lakes which were not believed to live in Slovenia. Near the village of Mota there is a large colony of grey heron, as well as many other birds living on the stagnant waters of gravel banks. The flood plains by the Ledava are overgrown with black alder woods, unknown elsewhere in Slovenia. The great changes which this Pannonian world will undergo in the near future, such as regulation of waters, water barriers, highway construction and the building of the railway line to Hungary, land improvement and the use of chemical agents in agriculture will bring a number of advantages as well as disadvantages.

12

13 Among other things, Ljutomer can pride itself on the horses it breeds for trotting races. The town has occupied the first rank in this sport for many years.

14 Before the Second World War there were no less than 94 mills on the fast-flowing Mura, wile today only the Babič floating mill (in the photograph) is left as an example. When there were no bridges yet across the Mura, ferry-boats were the only connection between Prekmurje and Štajerska.

15 Pomurje and Podravje are the home of the lucky bird, the white stork. Though people do take care not to disturb their nests, modern agriculture and the draining of wet meadows deprive them of food and reduce their chances to survive.

16 This mighty oak with a circumference of 675 cm grows on the Niederl farm in Spodnja Ščavnica.

17 Near Hrastovec in Slovenske gorice the old Hrastovec Castle, mentioned as early as the 13th century, occupies a precipice above the Pesnica valley. The name (hrast = oak) witnesses to the once vast oak forests. The renovated building today shows the appearance which it had in the 17th century. The diplomat Sigismund Herberstein (1486–1566) stayed at the castle on several occasions.

18 Slovenske gorice is a sub-Pannonian Tertiary hill range between the Drava and Mura rivers; to the west it stretches out into Austria, and to the south-east into the hills of Medjimurje in Croatia. Typically, the landscape is dotted with valleys, rounded hills, ridges, and settlements scattered on terraces. Vineyards and orchards occupy the sunny slopes, deciduous forests the shady slopes, meadows and pastures the wet valley floors, and fields the drained plains. Jeruzalem is a picturesque settlement in the eastern part of the hills of Ljutomer and Ormož.

18

Between the Paka and the Sotla River

The Šalek Valley, the Savinja Valley, the Celje basin, the Kozje region, the Sotla basin

The Celje basin is another typical natural junction of Slovenia. In terms of geology, the basin is surrounded in the north, west and south by fault lines. Only to the east is there a gradual transition into the Sotla region. In the Oligocene period, this territory was covered by the Pannonian Sea, which disappeared, leaving behind shoals, where plant remains continued to be deposited – today's coal and lignite. The western side of the basin is closed by the Dobrovlje plateau, an offshoot of the higher Menina. To the south are the mound-like mountains of the Posavje Hills, the highest being Čemšeniška planina (1,204 m), and other thousand metre peaks such as Kisovec (1,029 m) Mrzlica (1,122 m) and Gozdnik (1,090 m). In the north, the more remote 1,000-metre high mountains between Paški Kozjak and Boč form the horizon.

From a viewpoint at Boč (979 m), we can see that this mountain range divides the Drava and the Sava basins and continues rising to the north-west. The range consists of Konjiška gora (1,012 m), Stenica (1,091 m), Paški Kozjak (1,272 m), and a hint of Uršlja gora further up (1,699 m), which is already in the company of Alpine peaks. These mountains are actually an extension of the Karavanke range, which extends towards the east and slowly subsides into the hills of Croatian Slavonija. According to a new tectonic plate theory, the plate of this region joins the so-called 'Adriatic plate' and the continental Eurasian plate. That this is truly an area of fault lines is evidenced by a number of mineral and thermal water springs and the occasional earthquake.

While the old paths, roads and railways sought the lower-lying and thus more sinuous passages from the Drava to the Savinja basins, roadbuilding technology means that the new highway has taken a straight path. Driving from Maribor to Celje we witness a majestic show of nature in just a few minutes. At the high viaduct above the Dravinja, just before entering the tunnel, we can see the entire chain of the Karavanke foothills, while we leave behind the Pohorje of Alpine origin. In the tunnel we can suspect how perhaps here, deep below us in the earth's interior, new shifts in the earth's crust follow in the wake of forceful pressures of the hot earth. The shifts, hardly visible in the history of humankind, are, however, of great significance for the earth's evolution.

1 Before the Second World War Velenje was a small village near Šoštanj. The development of the mine, and the construction of a power plant and a white goods factory gave birth to a new town; nowadays, only the old castle above Velenje witnesses to the settlement of the valley in the Middle Ages. The oldest sections of the castle, which houses the Velenje Museum, are from the 13th century, and the Old Mine on Koroška cesta is the home of the Slovene Coal-mining Museum.

Left: The Žalec section of the Savinja Valley, with extensive fields of hops
Below: Location of aerial photograph shown on map 1 : 300 000

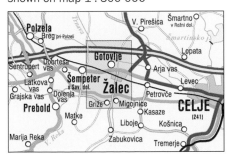

2 The Lower Savinja Valley is known for its advanced agriculture. In the 19th century the traditional crops were joined by hops, stimulated by the expanding brewery in Laško, which was established in 1825. The photograph shows hops and fields between Braslovče and Gora Oljka.

3 The Roman road from Ljubljana into the Celje basin passed over the Atrans (today Trojane) saddle. Later, the border between Carniola and Styria ran across the saddle and the hills of Posavje.

4 Boč is one of the best mountain viewpoints in Štajerska. Across the Drava plain we can see the Pohorje, to the north-east are Slovenske gorice, to the east Haloze and the nearby Donačka gora and Macelj, to the south-east Medvednica, to the south the hills of Kozjansko, behind them the Posavje hills, including Bohor and Lisca, and the Gorjanci hills. In clear weather Snežnik, the Julian Alps and the Kamnik and Savinja Alps are visible.

5 The Žiče monastery below Konjiška gora was the first Carthusian monastery to be founded in a non-Romance country. Its walls surround the monastic complex (under renovation), the church of St. John the Baptist (preserved walls) and a Gothic chapel.

6 At Celje, in the Church of St. Daniel, on the altar of the Chapel of the Sorrowful Mother of God, there is a pieta dating from about 1400.

The Celje area was settled in prehistory. In the Late Iron Age and early Antiquity, a Celto-Noric kingdom embraced this area as well. The Roman town of Celeia, present-day Celje, developed from a Celtic forerunner and had the status of a town *(municipium)*. The main Roman road towards Pannonia and the border on the Danube led through Celeia. In the hinterland of Celeia, at Šempeter, an important Roman necropolis was discovered which contained the tombs of Celeia's dignitaries and wealthy citizens. A catastrophic flood in the mid-3rd century buried the tombs in gravel. They were discovered in 1952 and can now be viewed at the excavation site.

Celje is one of the few Slovene towns to have preserved, to the present day, a link with ancient times. In the high and late Middle Ages, Celje was famous for its domestic feudal family of Celje Counts (the family line died out in 1456). Their residence was Stari grad near Celje, a magnificent building with a Romanesque core and later Gothic and Renaissance renovations. The castle was abandoned in the 17th century. The old road built by the Emperor Karl VI (in 1729), linking Vienna and Trieste, passed through Celje. The first train on the famous southern railway line arrived in Celje in 1846 from Vienna via Maribor.

The broader Celje region is known for its health spas. Archeological finds show that the springs at Laško and Rimske Toplice were already known by the Romans. The spa at Rogaška Slatina, known throughout Europe since the mid-19th century, was open even in the 17th century. The health spa displays many buildings in the classical style, while the modern buildings are somewhat less in tune with the rest.

Owing to its more remote location, the Kozjansko area became suitable for settlements which have survivied, such as Rifnik, Tinje near Žusem. The latest finds testify to an early settlement of the area by Slovenes.

History, not nature, drew the border along the Sotla river. Of the total length of 90 kilometres, 86 run along the present-day national border with Croatia. The frontier location between Austrian Styria and Hungarian Croatia is further illustrated by the many castles and old boroughs on both sides of the Sotla (Podčetrtek, Podsreda, Bistrica ob Sotli). The people on the Sotla did not recognize the river as the dividing line. To this attests the great Slovene-Croatian peasant uprising in 1573 and the subsequent joint resistance against the occupying forces during World War II. In order to preserve the memory of those days and the memory of the charismatic personality from the period of socialist Yugoslavia, fellow countryman Josip Broz 'Tito', Trebče Memorial Park was opened in 1981. Today this institution, called Kozjanski Park, and the Terme Olimia health spa near Podčetrtek are emerging as a centre of modern, environment-friendly development.

Used to the gently rolling hills and the sinuously curving rivers, we are astonished by the sharply cut gorge of the Bistrica between Trebče and Svete gore (Holy Mountains), where a group of churches have formed a pilgrimage site for centuries. Near Podčetrtek there is also Olimje Castle, which houses a 17th-century pharmacy.

7 One of the outstanding features of the Roman necropolis in Šempeter is the tomb of the Ennii. Particularly charming is the relief with a scene from Greek mythology – a bull (Zeus) carrying Europa on his back. The finds excavated in Šempeter are on view in situ.

8 Celje is a town on the Savinja and the third largest town of Slovenia. The Old Castle was the residence of the Counts of Celje in the Middle Ages.

9 Rogaška Slatina has a three-hundred-year-old tradition and is the oldest spa in Slovenia. The eminent buildings of the 19th century have been joined by modern ones. In the background Donačka gora.

10 The Rogaška glass-works, established in 1924, produce glass products of high quality and design.

11 After the turbulent peasant rebellions and the Second World War, Kozjansko, the area between the Voglajna and Sotla rivers, was a God-forgotten place for a long time. The Slovenes were reminded of its existence by the 1974 earthquake. Nowadays, traditions and culture, tourism and a modern spa together contribute to the area's progress. In the photograph: view of Donačka gora from Rifnik, an important archaeological site.

12 The church of St. Rocchus stands on an elevation above Šmarje pri Jelšah; its interior is richly decorated with wall paintings.

13 Podsreda Castle, first mentioned in 1213, stands on a precipice above Podsreda. It is the seat of the Kozjansko Park. The castle has regular opening hours; it has a permanent glass exhibition and installs numerous occasional exhibitions.

11

12

13

Down the Sava River

The Sava Valley between Ljubljana and Brežice, the Posavje Hills

The Sava is a kind of diagonal of Slovenia and marks the dividing line between the north-east and south-west. From Zagorje to Jesenice in Dolenjska, the Sava has been an age-long divide between the former provinces of Styria and Carniola.

At Zasavje and Posavje (the valley of the Sava and the land on both banks between Litija and Zidani Most, or Zidani Most and Brežice) two characteristic, yet invisible geographical lines intersect: the 15th meridian of eastern longitude, according to which Central European Time is set, cuts through Zagorje; and the 46th parallel of north latitude, passing through Brestanica and the Sava near Sevnica. Both lines meet at Gabrovka in Dolenjska. In 1982, geodesists determined the exact geometrical center of Slovenia (GEOSS), which is at Spodnja Slivna above Vače, with the two following geographical coordinates: $\lambda = 14°48'55,2"$ and $\psi = 46°07'11,8"$.

The River Sava (the name derives from the antique form of Savus, which probably derives from another, older name) was an important watercourse even in pre-historic times. Legend has it that Jason and the Argonauts navigated upstream. However, there was navigation on the river in the Roman period. For the animals which helped pull the boats upstream, a path was cut into the narrow passage above Zidani Most, which can still be seen today in places where it was cut into the bedrock. Until the opening of the railway line between Celje and Ljubljana, the ferries on the Sava were important economically in this Slovene region. After 1848, when cargo was transferred to the railroad, the ferry service between Zidani Most and Ljubljana soon vanished. With the construction of the railway between Zidani Most and Zagreb in 1862, transportation links for the entire Posavje region were provided.

Zidani Most, the present-day railway and road intersection, is a fine example of how important it was to build passages over natural barriers such as a large river. The place received its name after the first stone bridge across the Sava (at a site opposite the railway station), which was commissioned in 1224 by Duke Leopold the Famous. The bridge has been gone for a long time. Of the present three bridges, none crosses the Sava. They are all built over the Savinja. The oldest road bridge goes back to 1848, and is followed by the stone railway bridge (1847–49) and finally, the reinforced concrete railway bridge (finished in 1931).

The first settlements in Zasavje are from the Late Stone, Copper and Bronze Ages. However, fortified settlements on the hills proliferated only in the Iron

1 The area north-east of Vače is one of the most eminent archaeological sites of the Hallstatt period in Slovenia; the most exquisite excavated object is the figurally ornamented Vače situla. The original situla is in the National Museum in Ljubljana, but an enlarged copy is exhibited in the village of Klenik near Vače.

Left: The Kompolje section of the Sava valley between Radeče and Sevnica
Below: Location of aerial photograph shown on map 1 : 300 000

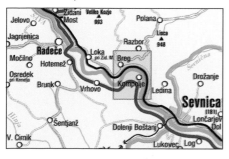

2 The geometrical centre of Slovenia (GEOSS) at Spodnja Slivna in the Posavje hills is marked by an upright square stone block made of Pohorje tonalite, bearing the national coat-of-arms and the contours of Slovenia. The monument is completed by a flagpole with Slovenia' s flag and a linden tree. After 1991 GEOSS became a popular excursion destination and the venue of popular gatherings.

3 Bogenšperk Castle was once owned by Johann Weichard Valvasor (1641–93), a traveller and expert on Carniola and the neighbouring provinces, which he described extensively. Here he wrote *Die Ehre des Herzogthums Crain* (The Glory of the Duchy of Carniola), a 3532-page "encyclopaedia" in 15 volumes with 528 illustrations and 24 supplements, which was published in Nürnberg in 1689. Valvasor had his own copperplate printing works at Bogenšperk, the first one of its kind in Slovenia.

4 Near Litija, a small textile and wood processing centre in the Sava Valley, the river makes a sweeping bend around the small fertile plain created by its deposits, and then flows through a narrow gorge.

5 A memorial to coal miners before the Hrastnik colliery, by Stojan Batič.

Age. On the saddle between the Sava and Moravče valleys, the prosperous Iron-Age center of Vače developed. This is also the site of one of the most important archaeological finds, with numerous burial sites and a strongly fortified settlement. Vače is known throughout the world for the famous find of an Illyrian situla dating to around 800 BC. The bronze bucket is decorated with three belts of friezes, and can be seen at the National Museum of Slovenia in Ljubljana. Another important Iron-Age settlement, although somewhat overshadowed by Vače, is at Libna, near Krško. In the Late Iron Age, people began to settle the lowlands (Dobova, Brežice) as well as the northern fringes of the Gorjanci range.

A Celtic settlement and later a Roman town, the new town of Neviodunum, lay on the plain by the Sava and was a major river port. The foundations of buildings and some river wharf structures near the village of Drnovo have survived. In the Middle Ages and later, it was predominantly the banks of the Sava that were settled. Thus, market towns sprang up around feudal castles, which later grew into towns, such as Radeče, Krško, and Brežice. Brestanica, the former Rajhenburg, only achieved the status of a market town despite the old Romanesque castle. The Rajhenburg castle served as a camp for Slovene war deportees from Štajerska during the German occupation.

For centuries, with the exception of the medieval bridge across the Sava at Zidani Most, no other bridges were built in the valley. Cargo and people traversed the river by ferry. At important crossing points market towns sprang up such as Sevnica. It developed in the immediate vicinity of a feudal castle on the neighbouring hill. Also surviving as an attachment to the castle is the so-called *Lutrovska klet* (Lutheran Cellar), where Jurij Dalmatin preached during the Reformation. Sevnica received early mention in 1275, and as a market town in 1309. In the hinterland, on the sunny slopes of the left bank of the Sava Valley, lies the site of the late Roman fortified settlement of Ajdovski gradec, near Vranje.

The Zasavje and Posavje regions are important industrial centres. Coal started to be mined in the middle of the 19th century. Good quality brown coal and the proximity of the railway resulted in the rapid development of the district. The villages turned into the mining towns of Trbovlje, Zagorje and Hrastnik. Coal deposits were later discovered at the foot of Bohor where, after the First World War, the mine of Senovo developed. Senovo used to be connected with nearby Brestanica ob Savi by a narrow-gauge railroad. Steam power stations were built in Zasavje and at Senovo, which added to the excessive pollution of the narrow valley. By the Sava near Krško the first nuclear, and in terms of capacity, the biggest power plant in Slovenia was built.

The concentration of mining and industry in Zasavje gave rise to the first proletarian and trade union movement, but also brought about inestimable devastation of the environment.

▶

6 The old Sevnica Castle is a typical medieval, rectangular fortress with four corner towers. The predecessor of the present-day castle, which dates from the 17th century, was mentioned as early as 1309, but it was probably even older. It stands on a hill above the market and commands the Sava Valley.

7 Brežice Castle is a Renaissance fortress with four wings enclosing a spacious courtyard. The first mention of it dates from 1249. Baroque rebuilt in 1699, it was enlarged with the biggest secular Baroque room with a mirror ceiling in Slovenia. The hall is painted with motifs from Ovid's *Metamorphoses* and similar scenes, which have no match anywhere near. The hall is used for concerts.

8 For several decades archaeologists have been working on Ajdovski gradec near Vranje above Sevnica, one of the biggest Early Christian centres of the whole Alpine and Danubian area. They have excavated remains of two Early Christian basilicas, a baptistery, and other remains of the fading Roman era in the territory of present-day Slovenia.

9 Terme Čatež are the biggest natural spa in Slovenia.

10 Mokrice Castle is another example of the huge castle architecture of the Posavje region's lower end. The massive centre of the castle was built in the 16th century in defence against the Turkish incursions, and was later adapted to the needs of its feudal residents. The adjacent extensive park (18,5 ha) was protected as a "monument of designed nature" in 1951. The building has been turned into a high-class hotel with its own golf course.

8

9

10

The Rolling Hills and the Dreamy Streams of Dolenjska

The Dolenjska Hills, Suha Krajina, the Mirna Valley, the Krško Plain, the Gorjanci

1 The Cistercian abbey of Stična was first mentioned in 1136. In 1784 the monastery was abandoned, to be reoccupied by monks after more than a century. The Romanesque, three-nave basilica is a precious monument. Stična was an important centre of culture in the Middle Ages, a function now continued by the Slovene Religious Museum.

Left: Kostanjevica-on-Krka, a little island town
Below: Location of aerial photograph shown on map 1 : 300 000

South of the Sava, yet still within the range of the Posavje Hills, lies the only high mountain, Kum (1,220 m), reaching even higher than its neighbours on the left bank of the Sava. Further south, the landscape becomes more gentle in the rolling hills and valleys of Dolenjska, reaching as far as the hills of the Kočevje area and the Gorjanci range. Large areas of Dolenjska are karstic. Almost all the headwaters of Dolenjska's largest river, the Krka (94 km), are concentrated at a single site. Except for the Višnjica there are no other tributaries, but there are several strong karst springs near the river. The Krka presents two aspects. From its source to Otočec, where it still has a considerable gradient, it jumps over tufa thresholds and dams, and calms down in green pools. The upper valley closely follows the fault line in the Dinaric direction, and while the Krka swerves away towards Novo mesto, the fault line continues along the Valley of Radeščica and Črmošnjice to Bela krajina. Below Soteska, the valley widens a little, and at Meniška vas the Krka swings left at right angles and catches up with the second fault line along the south end of the Krško polje (the Krško Plain), which it follows until its confluence with the Sava. Below Struga, its gradient lessens significantly, and the river widens, meandering slowly through Krško polje. The second in size is the non-karstic Mirna, whose waters gather in the hills of Dolenjska and join the Sava at Boštanj.

The Krško polje depression formed in the mid-Miocene period, about 15 million years ago, and was later flooded by the Pannonian Sea. At the end of the Tetiary the sea marl sediments, which in places abound in fossilised snails and shells, were covered with flint sandstone, deposits of ancient rivers in the sea bay. Finally, gravel was deposited in the eastern part of the basin by the Sava in the Ice Age and later. In the Quaternary period the tributaries from the hills on the northern fringes of Krško polje deposited a layer of impermeable clay, unsuitable for cultivating. There remains a lowland oak forest, Krakovski gozd, as a green oasis amid the well-tended fields.

Krško polje is an active tectonic area. This is confirmed by the warm water springs bursting from the ground at the fault line under the Gorjanci: at one end are the hot springs of the Čatež Thermal Spa and, at the other end, the hot springs of Dolenjske Toplice, with some more hot springs in between at

2 The historical centre of Mirna spreads around the church of St. John the Baptist on the right bank of the Mirna river. First mentioned in 1265, the church was rebuilt several times; the frescoes in the church date from 1463–65.

3 This 13th-century Romanesque ossuary was built into the slope near the church of St. James above Gorenji Mokronog. It is one of the few medieval ossuaries preserved in Slovenia and the only one in Dolenjska.

4 The double hayrack (*kozolec*) of the Dolenjska type may be a strictly functional outbuilding, but it is nevertheless often embellished with delicate wooden ornament. The hayrack in the photograph stands in Muljava.

5 The birth-place of the writer Josip Jurčič in Muljava has been turned into a museum.

6 Žužemberk Castle was destroyed by allied planes in March 1945. It is still in ruins, except for one renovated defence tower from the 16th century.

7 The village of Soteska on the left bank of the Krka was the site of a mighty castle. Only the outer walls and the garden pavilion have survived. The two thickest known elm trees in Slovenia grow by the Krka.

8 The provost Chapter Church of St. Nicholas is the dominant feature of Novo mesto; first mentioned in 1428. Adorning the main altar is the oil painting of the patron saint, St. Nicholas, the work of the Venetian mannerist Jacopo **Robusti, known as Tintoretto. Metzinger's** works adorn the **two lateral altars.**

Kostanjevica. The extensive mountain ridge of Gorjanci was formed when the ground did not subside. The shady areas on the Slovene side are overgrown with forests and unpopulated. The highest peak, Trdinov vrh (1,178 m), lies on the state border. Beneath it lie the last remnants of the Gorjanci virgin forest.

Like other fertile regions, Dolenjska was settled early, beginning in the Late Stone Age. Numerous dwellings and fortified prehistoric sites are scattered throughout the region. The most famous are the Hallstatt culture sites on Magdalenska gora above Šmarje, and at Stična, Novo mesto and Šmarjeta, where rich burial finds, especially situlas, were discovered. The Romans settled along the main routes connecting Emona and Siscia (Sisak) with smaller outposts (Praetorium Latobicorum near Trebnje) and towns (Neviodunum – Drnovo near Krško). In late Antiquity, the fortified settlement of Velike Malence was built close to the confluence of the Sava and the Krka.

In the Middle Ages, the inhabitants of Dolenjska concentrated around feudal castles (Višnja Gora, Žužemberk, Otočec) and original parish centres (Šentvid pri Stični) and along its borders. At the time, the greater part of the Novo mesto district belonged to so-called 'Slovenska krajina' (the Slovene borderland), which became part of Carniola only in the 13th century.

The early towns of Dolenjska later started to lag behind. Thus, for example, Višnja Gora was mentioned as a market town in the second half of the 14th century, and obtained the status of a town in 1478. Even older is Kostanjevica, recorded as market town in 1249 and as town in 1252, and in 1215 minted its own currency. A fierce competitor was Otok pri Drami (Gutenwerth), which, however, was destroyed and deserted during Turkish raids. The remains of the town were excavated no more than two decades ago. A relatively young medieval settlement was Novo mesto, which was granted municipal rights by the Austrian Archduke Rudolf IV in 1365. In his honour, the town was named Rudolfovo (Rudolfswerth), but finally the popular name for it, Novo mesto, was adopted. It became the economic and cultural centre of the Dolenjska region.

There are three famous monasteries in Dolenjska: Stična, Pleterje, and Kostanjevica. They each followed their own path of development, yet their histories have a common point: medieval flourishing, decline, and later revival.

The transversal connection of the central Dolenjska and Zasavje runs through the valley of Mirna (Mirnska dolina). Only a low elevation separates it from the Temenica, which was easily overcome by the railway line, built just before the Second World War, connecting Trebnje with Sevnica.

The third famous Slovene wine-producing district is the Posavje-Bela krajina region, also including the vineyards of Dolenjska. Scattered on sunny slopes are the grape varieties of *Žametna Črnina* (Black Velvet), *Modra Frankinja*, *Portugalka* or *Kraljevina*. A blend of these varieties yields a light, sour, drinkable wine called *Rdeči Cviček*. According to connoisseurs, the home of authentic *Cviček* is Gadova Peč under the Gorjanci.

The traffic in Dolenjska ran along a medieval road with many steep gradients. Progress came with the railway line, which in 1893 provided the connection between Novo mesto and Ljubljana, and was later, in 1914, extended via Bela krajina to Karlovac. The main road, built in 1985, can no longer handle the growing traffic flowing from western Europe through the Balkans and on to the Middle East.

9 Most of the Krka's picturesque tufa rapids are between Žužemberk and Dvor. On some of them dams for mills and sawmills were constructed.

10 Novo mesto, the centre of Dolenjska, occupied a strategic elevation in a bend of the Krka already in the Middle Ages.

11 The left bank of the Krka near Kostanjevica and the Ljubljana-Zagreb road enclose the biggest flood-plain oak forest in Slovenia. Relatively well preserved, it has an area of 40.5 hectares, and was protected as a secondary primeval forest in 1952. The pedunculate oaks are up to 300 years old and up to 40 m high. (A fine example is Cvelbar's oak near Malence: its circumference is 699 cm and its height is 27 m high.)

12 Kostanjevica na Krki stands on an elaborately designed island in the middle of the Krka. The settlement started to develop in the 13th century, is mentioned as a town in 1252, and was granted special privileges in 1300. The parish church of St. James has a Romanesque portal; the former ministerial mansion from the late 15th century houses the Lamut Art Gallery. The nearby Kostanjevica cave is worth a visit.

13 The second Cistercian monastery in Dolenjska was founded in Kostanjevica in 1234 as a defence post against Hungarian incursions. It was the largest Baroque monastic complex in Slovenia with ranges of arcaded corridors and an exceptional architecture of its Early Gothic church.
After the dissolution the buildings deteriorated, but were carefully renovated after 1945. The renovated wings house the Božidar Jakac Gallery. A permanent exhibition of Forma Viva wooden sculptures is installed in the open air.

14 Globodol is a hidden, 4-km-long and largely dry karst *polje*, located at a distance from the main roads which connect Suha krajina and the Temenica valley; the biggest of the three settlements is Gorenji Globodol.

15 The Pleterje Charterhouse was founded by Count Hermann II of Celje in 1407. During the following centuries the monastery changed owners several times, to be dissolved by the Emperor Joseph II. In 1899 it was restored to the Carthusian order, which renovated and rebuilt it in 1900–05. The medieval structure has been preserved in part (church, sacristy, wine cellar, remains of the chapter wing and the refectory). The monastery has an open-air museum at the Šmarje-Vratno road.

Forests, and more forests ...

Lašče, the Ribnica Valley, Loški potok, the Kočevje region, Rog, the Upper Kolpa Valley

1 Turjak Castle sits on a steep rock promontory above the Želimlje valley; it was started in the 13th century and was one of the most eminent castles in the

1 Turjak Castle sits on a steep rock promontory above the Želimlje valley; it was started in the 13th century and was one of the most eminent castles in the

former Carniola. The castle was the residence of one of the most powerful feudal dynasties in Carniola, the Auersperg or Turjak family. They were notable politicians and leading industrialists, who supported writers, including Trubar, Dalmatin, and Finžgar. The history of the castle inspired both Jurčič and Prešeren. In the autumn of 1943 the castle – at that time a stronghold of the White Guard – was attacked by the Partisans and severely damaged; it is now partially renovated and can be visited. An old linden tree grows in front of the castle.

Left: Kočevje with environs
Below: Location of aerial photograph shown on map 1 : 300 000

South of Turjak, the site of an 13th-century castle and an important crossroads for the Ljubljana basin, there begins a small region which is geographically part of Dolenjska, but the local people affiliate themselves neither with the region of Dolenjska, nor that of Notranjska. The region is named Kočevsko (the Kočevje region) after a former county and its largest town, although it is composed of at least five distinct geographical units: Lašče, the Ribnica Valley, Kočevje, Loški potok and Kostel, including the upper Kolpa Valley. Much of the region is inhabited.

With a few exceptions (the vicinity of Lašče, Slemena, the Upper Kolpa), this is the Dinaric karst, where all rivers at some point flow beneath the earth's surface. North of Ribnica they flow to the Krka, and south of Ribnica to the Kolpa basin. Between Mala gora and Velika gora (Turn, 1,254 m) lies the (karstic) Ribnica polje with the old market town of Ribnica, which is the oldest settlement in the entire area. The plain is supplied with water by the Bistrica and the Ribnica. The juncture between the Ribnica and Kočevje basins is at Jasnica, with the sinking creek of Rinža. The Kočevje basin is flanked on three sides by vast forests: Stojna, Kočevska Mala gora, and the extensive Rog. Despite a modern road, the picturesque Kolpa Valley, with the old castle of Kostel, which played an important role in the defense of Carniola against the Turks, is still believed to be rather remote. To ensure better protection, Kočevje was encircled by a wall, and in 1471 obtained municipal rights. Besides Bela krajina, the regions of Kočevje, Ribnica and Notranjska suffered greatly under Turkish forays into the area. News of impending danger was spread by beacons lit on the higher peaks, such as St. Ana (932 m), near Ribnica, and Grmada (887 m), above Velike Poljane.

Kočevsko boasts a unique history, including the 600 years of the *Kočevarji*, the German inhabitants of the area who were brought to the region by the feudal lords in the 14th century. Almost all of them emigrated in November 1941 on Hitler's orders. The poor soil could not provide a living, which is why the *Kočevarji* were also peddlers. The Austrian government helped them by founding a German high school in Kočevje and connecting the town with Ljubljana in 1893 by railway. The resourceful inhabitants of Ribnica

2 Ribnica Castle was first mentioned in the 13th century. It was occupied by a range of feudal lords; the last one was the Rudež family, who lived in the castle from the early 19th century onwards. During the Second World War the castle was burned down and later partially renovated. The courtyard features a memorial park dedicated to important figures from Ribnica (among others the composer Jacobus Gallus, the linguist Stanislav Škrabec, the cartographer Peter Kozler, the Slavic scholar Ivan Prijatelj, and the politician Janez Evangelist Krek). The castle houses the collections of the Ribnica Museum

3 The Ribnica Valley is a world of its own between the hills of Velika gora and Mala gora. Every first Sunday of September Ribnica is the scene of the traditional Ribnica fair, a parade of wooden utensils. Utensils made by cottage craftsmen are the most popular souvenirs.

4 The church of the Assumption in Nova Štifta stands on a panoramic ledge overlooking the Ribnica Valley. Built in 1641, it became a model for this type of Baroque architecture in Slovenia. Several old, bushy linden trees grow near the church.

5 The Temko mill at Rašica. The mill counts as the home of Primož Trubar, the father of the standard literary Slovene language. The mill's present appearance dates from the 19th century; on the occasion of the 400th anniversary of Trubar's death it was renovated, and a permanent exhibition about Trubar's life and work was installed. A memorial to Trubar was erected nearby in 1952, on the 400th anniversary of the first book printed in Slovene

6 Velike Lašče, a major settlement at the Škofljica-Kočevje regional road, was first mentioned in 1145. The two-tower church of Our Lady's Birth from the 19th century is an impressive monument. The *Pri Kuklju* inn exhibits personal belongings of the famous local writers, Fran Levstik (born in nearby Dolnje Retje) and Josip Stritar (born in Podsmreka pri Velikih Laščah), their books and other books. The ceiling in the "black kitchen" dates from 1778. A bust of the writer and poet Jože Javoršek stands at the entrance to the inn. A memorial to Fran Levstik was erected in the main square in 1889.

supplemented their earnings with pottery, and especially woodenware, which they peddled in every corner of the Austrian Empire. Three hundred and six hectares of the virgin forest at Kočevski Rog were set aside after 1888 to preserve what remained of the wilderness for posterity. These were the first nature reserves in Slovenia and in former Yugoslavia, and have largely been maintained until now. During the Liberation War the forests of Kočevje were the unconquerable bastion of the partisans hiding in their recesses, after 1942, the leadership of the resistance, as well as hospitals, a printing facility, bunkers, and the communications system were all located there. Sadly, Kočevski Rog and several other sites after the Second World War became a mass grave for thousands of captured soldiers, predominantly Slovene and Croatian homeguards, ustasha and chetniks, who wittingly or unwittingly found themselves on the side of the aggressor and were liquidated here without judicial examination. A reconciliation ceremony in July 1990 was intended to close this chapter of Slovenian history.

7 Loški potok is a bowl-shaped dry karst valley *(uvala),* divided into two by the saddle containing the Hrib-Loški potok settlement. There are characteristic fields alligned in rows.

8 The Upper Kolpa Valley widens just a little around the Croatian village of Brod and the Slovene Vas and Fara. In the Middle Ages this important passage across the Kolpa was under the control of Kostel Castle, built on top of a steep rock face.

9 Kočevski Rog is a 35-km-long and 15-km-wide plateau-like, forested mountain range (part of the Dinaric Alps), bordered by the Kočevje plain to the west, and Suha krajina to the north-west; to the east it extends into the Črmošnjica valley and Bela krajina, and in the south Poljanska gora, part of Kočevski Rog, reaches the Kolpa. Typical features are the abundant karst collapse caves, caves and abysses, as well as giant trees. The main historical monuments are the Partisan field hospitals and the mass graves of members of the Slovene Home Guard and of other Yugoslav nations, who were executed here after the Second World War.

10 The Nežica stream rises in several forks in a head valley above the Kolpa Valley, near Fara. Right above the Kočevje-Brod na Kupi road the stream forms the 15-m-high Tišenpolj waterfall, also called Nežica, which is one of the rare waterfalls in south-eastern Slovenia.

11 The precipitous edges of Borovška gora above the left bank of the Kolpa river reach a relative height of 700 m. The picture shows Loška stena (Ložec face), part of Borovška gora.

12 Kočevje is an urban settlement in the southern part of the Kočevje plain, on the Rinža river; to the west rises Stojna, to the east Kočevska Mala gora. Kočevje is the economic, administrative, cultural, and education centre of the Kočevje region. The settlement probably originated in close connection with the German colonisation in the first third of the 14th century. In October 1943 it was the venue of the Assembly of the Delegates of the Slovene Nation. The area of the former coal-mine is now covered by a lake. The town is home to the Regional Museum, and the nearby Željnske jame caves are quite interesting.

13 Kočevski Rog was a forest bastion, in which a major part of the partisan army found refuge. The Baza 20 camp is a popular excursion destination. Most of its renovated buildings have their original appearance; the road to the camp starts in the Črmošnjice valley.

14 The small church of St. Egidius stands at the edge of the village of Ribjek near Osilnica. The interior is partially decorated with wall paintings, and the gilded high altar dates from 1681.

Vineyards and Birch Trees

Bela krajina, the Poljanska dolina Valley, the Lower Kolpa Valley

One does not simply enter Bela krajina, but is gradually drawn into it. Bela krajina can be reached from the north by the old road running over the Vahta pass (615 m), and more recently by way of the so-called *Partizanska magistrala* (the "Partisan main road"), passing the Črmošnjice Valley and descending towards Bela krajina at Brezje (538 m). But the most surprising arrival in the region is provided by the Novo mesto railway. Emerging from an almost 2-km long tunnel, we find ourselves overlooking the Semič vineyards, high above the entire region of Bela krajina. From the southern, Croatian side, the region can be accessed by two roads crossing the borderline River Kolpa, at Metlika and Vinica. The bend of the Kolpa at Damelj is located at 45° 25' north, which is also the southernmost tip of Slovenia. This means that Slovenia lies in the northern half of the northern hemisphere, closer to the North Pole than to the Equator.

1 Bela krajina outclasses all the other Slovene provinces in terms of folk traditions, dances, costumes, and customs. What is the origin of this variety? The old cultural heritage was enriched by the Uskoki, refugees from the Turkish provinces, who settled in the then Military Zone along the Kolpa. – Some of their traditions have been preserved for folklore and tourist events. The picture shows *Zeleni Jurij*, literally "the green George" – a spring ritual.

If one had to single out one natural feature of Bela krajina, it would be the formations of lowland karst. The impermeable rocks, marl, and clay deposited in the gulf of the long-vanished Pannonian Sea prevented water from seeping through the ground and finding its way across the limestone hinterland towards the Kolpa. The karst waters remained trapped not far from the surface, feeding the Lahinja's tributaries.

The biggest of these numerous karst springs is the Krupa, which comes gushing to the surface in a picturesque pool at the foot of the towering rock face at Stranska vas. With its meandering course and dreamy pace, gentle gradient and densely overgrown banks, the Lahinja is a typical Bela krajina river. But we do not want to overlook the 294-km long Kolpa. The 116 kilometres of its course between Osilnica and the mouth of the Kamenica stream follow the national border. Another interesting feature of the Kolpa is that its headwaters, which eventually flow into the Black Sea, are closest to the Adriatic. Its karst continental divide is only 10.4 km as the crow flies from the Gulf of Bakar.

Left: The Lahinja meanders near the village of Butoraj in Bela krajina
Below: Location of aerial photograph shown on map 1 : 300 000

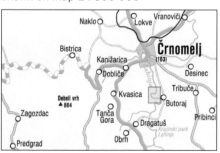

For Slovenians living in one of the central regions of Slovenia, Bela krajina seems quite a remote region, although it is only an hour-and-a half's drive from Ljubljana. When in September 1943 Italy capitulated, a liberated territory was formed in Bela krajina by the Partisans; they retained their position until the

2 Birches and ferns on clay soil are Bela krajina's *steljniki*. They resulted from the extensive agriculture in the past, when quite everything which the poor soil could offer was used to survive. This landscape is the symbol of Bela krajina, reminding visitors and natives of the hard, and yet rewarding peasant life in former times.

3 Bela krajina is a region in the south-east of Slovenia, bordered by Kočevski Rog, Poljanska gora, the Gorjanci Hills, and the Kolpa river. It is a hilly landscape, full of sink-holes, and other karst phenomena, and largely green. In the photograph: cultural landscape near Semič.

4 Relief of Mithras, cut into the bedrock in the forest near the village of Rožanec, 3rd century AD. Votive inscription, scene of the sacrifice of the sacred bull.

5 Picturesque karst spring of the Krupa, south-east of Semič. The water emerges from under a 60-m-high precipitous rock face and has around 11 °C at the source.

6 Metlika is the urban, economic, administrative, and cultural centre of the north-eastern part of Bela krajina. A castle housing the Bela krajina Museum and the Slovene Firemen's Museum stands right above the town, and the big adjacent building once was a commendam belonging to the Knights of the Cross.

end of the war despite two 'home-guard' attacks. Less than a half century ago, however, Bela krajina became the central Slovene region for a year and a half. This is where the national, cultural and scientific institutions of the future Republic of Slovenia were conceived.

Bela krajina boasts a long and varied history. Archeological finds at Pusti gradec, Kučar near Podzemelj and Vinomer are testimonies of human presence in prehistoric times, from the Copper to the Iron Age. In the Roman period, two Roman outposts were located at the site of present-day Črnomelj and Metlika. A Roman road led from the Krka Valley to Sisak via Metlika. The Romans left behind an unusual outdoor monument which has not changed in 1,700 years, a mithreum near the village of Rožanec. It shows a relief of the god Mithras sacrificing a bull, carved into a rock in a small karst depression. Bela krajina is also a rare ethnological treasure chest of Slovenia.

5

6

7 Knights of the German Order erected three churches, called Tri fare ("Three Parishes") at the edge of the village of Rosalnica, probably in the mid 12th century. The present buildings are from the 14th and 15th centuries and are among the most important monuments of sacral architecture in Bela krajina.

8 Gradac is a cluster village on both banks of a meander of the Lahinja; it is the site of the home castle of the Grätzer aristocrats, rebuilt in the 17th century. The Red Cross of Slovenia was founded in the former Sokol house in June 1944.

9 The sources of the Lahinja and Nerajčica were protected as a landscape park, drawing attention to this interesting natural and relatively well preserved part of Bela krajina's karst peneplain, where the natural and cultural heritage blend.

10 Črnomelj, first mentioned in 1228, is the biggest urban settlement of Bela krajina and the traffic, economic, administrative, and cultural centre of the region. It is located at the junction of the roads from Dolenjske Toplice, Metlika, Vinica, Stari trg ob Kolpi, and Adlešiči; and it is also on the Ljubljana-Metlika railway line. The town's principal cultural heritage is the castle, the building of the German Order of the Cross, and the churches of St. Peter and the Holy Spirit.

11 The remains of Vinica Castle are on a high terrace above the Kolpa; the building's core dates from the 15th century. The Oton Zupančič Memorial House in Vinica exhibits the writer's library and memorial collection, and an ethnological collection. A memorial room, dedicated to the academician Dr. Oton Berkopec, is also arranged in the same house.

12 Stari trg ob Kolpi is a cluster settlement in the Poljanska dolina Valley, located on a steep promontory above the Kolpa. Roads from the settlement lead to Kočevje, Vinica and, along the Kolpa, to Kostel.

11

12

Notranjska Presents Herself

The Postojna basin, the Pivka, Notranjska poljes, Bloke, the Snežnik range, the Javorniki

1 The first section of a motorway in Slovenia, between Vrhnika and Postojna, was opened in 1972. Nowadays, the network of motorways is in full expansion.

Left: Otok (Island) in the south-western corner of Lake Cerknica
Below: Location of aerial photograph shown on map 1 : 300 000

From the geographical point of view, Notranjska is the most typical Dinaric region of Slovenia. It has all the characteristics of a karst region, yet it is different from the karst of Primorje. Abundant rain and snow fall on the limestone and dolomite surface of the mountains and plateaus of the Notranjska region, yet all this water vanishes into the ground and resurfaces on the fringes of the lower-lying poljes (karst fields) and dolines (sinks). The entire region of Notranjska is a large, intricate, hydro-geological system, known for its underground water system called the Kraška Ljubljanica. Today's lost rivers, separated on the surface, yet connected underground, a million years ago constituted a single river basin, which sent its rivers towards the Ljubljana Marshes. The main part of the waters of the Kraška Ljubljanica are the two forks embracing the high plateaus and peaks of the Snežnik and Javornik ranges.

The western, the Pivka fork, has its source at the village of Zagorje as a rather weak, irregular spring. The true river bed with a permanent flow of water begins only in the Pivka basin. The only larger tributary of the Pivka is the Nanoščica, which joins the Pivka near Postojna, while the neighbouring Lokva stream, which sinks into the Predjama Castle Cave, belongs to the water system of the Vipava. Thus the continental divide between the Adriatic Sea and the Black Sea runs right across the Pivka basin. The Pivka continues its course through the world-famous cave of Postojnska jama, hiding from view for several kilometres, and reappears in the Pivka fork of Planinska jama (the Planina Cave).

The second fork, traversing the poljes (karst fields) of Notranjska, adopts an even more unusual course. Its source is on the Croatian side as the Trbuhovica stream. It then goes underground at Babno polje only to surface as Veliki Obrh in the valley of the Loška dolina. After a short stretch, the stream again sinks below ground near the village of Dane and resurfaces after a few kilometres in the Cerknica polje (Cerkniško polje) as the Stržen. The Cerknica polje is the reservoir of the waters descending from the Javorniki and Bloke. A part of the Bloke water has cut a route through the cave of Križna jama, one of the most magnificent water caves in the world. The Cerkniščica is another stream which feeds the Cerknica polje.

When, in the rainy season, all these waters come rushing to the Cerknica polje, the sink holes and swallow holes can not handle the over-abundant volume of water and the result is the seasonal Lake Cerknica (Cerkniško jezero), during its existence the largest continental water surface in Slovenia.

▶

2 Emerging from the Planina Cave (Planinska jama) is the Unica river, which results from the subterranean confluence of the Pivka and Rak forks within the Planina cave, additionally fed by the subterranean waters of the Javorniki.

3 The Planina polje, with the second biggest periodic lake in Slovenia, is about 6 km long and has a maximum width of 3.5 km. Water flows onto it from the Planina cave and the sources of the Malenščica; the Unica river then flows across the plain in numerous meanders, to completely disappear from the porous limestone surface by way of around 150 small and big *ponors* and caves.

4 Lake Cerknica, presumably called *Lacus Lugeus* in the Roman era, attracted Valvasor's attention because it keeps disappearing and reappearing mysteriously on the Cerknica polje. His research of the lake earned him membership in the British Royal Society in 1687. When it is a lake, it is visited by swarms of water birds.

5 The chapel of Predjama Castle contains a stone Pietà from early 15th century.

The surface area of the lake may cover as many as 24 km^2, while its depth is only a few metres. The underground outflow from the lake follows several directions. The longest subterranean channel leads to the sources at Bistra on the edge of Ljubljansko Barje (the Ljubljana Marshes). Another part of the water flows from caves on the edge of the lake to the Planinsko polje, and the third part surfaces over a short stretch in the nearby Rakov Škocjan. The valley of the Rak stream is an unpredictable feature amid the forest-covered plateaus. It is a veritable collection of superb Karst formations, such as the source cave of Zelška jama, sinking Tkalca jama, two natural bridges and much, much more. From the Rakov Škocjan the waters run along a subterranean riverbed to Planinska jama (the Planina Cave), where they join the Pivka coming from the Postojna Cave and then jointly spring from the ground at Planinsko polje as the Unica. Upstream, the Unica is a fast river; it then calms down to become a scenic river meandering over the Planinsko polje, sinking at its farther edge. The Planinsko polje is also an intermittent lake, perhaps even more picturesque than Lake Cerknica, but its waters remain on the surface for only a short period. In the downstream section of the underground Unica, which is soon to be renamed as the Ljubljanica, the waters from the Logatec polje and Rovte increase its volume, and the river finally surfaces at Vrhnika as the Ljubljanica. Here, the karst underworld ends.

The formation of the Notranjska poljes (karst fields) is undoubtedly connected with the great tectonic fault which was mentioned in connection with Idrija. The fault line runs along the Hotedrščica, passing through the Planina polje, Cerknica polje, and Loška dolina polje to Prezid, and on to the valley of the Čabranka.

The Snežnik mountain range attains a height of about 1,000 metres, with the highest peak, Snežnik (1,796 m), as the tallest non-alpine mountain in Slovenia. In addition to a panoramic view, which encompasses Venice, the Carnic Alps, the Julian Alps, and the Karavanke and Pohorje, Snežnik boasts several natural curiosities. The peak, which, due to its exposed location, reaches well above the timber line, is a meeting point of Alpine and Balkan plant and animal life, which rarely occur in such close proximity. Also of interest are the nearby ice caves, dry caves and pits.

Notranjska is an excellent example of the importance of communication for the development of a region. The Cerknica polje and the Bloke plateau were settled in prehistory. In the Middle Ages a trade route led through Bloke, connecting the region of Dolenjska with the Adriatic sea. In the Roman period, Cerknica was a stopover on the road leading from Emona to the coast and was granted municipal rights in the 11th century. Stari trg and Lož, two ancient settlements, developed along the old route through the Lož Valley (Loška dolina). Lož obtained municipal rights in 1477 thanks to its proximity to the border. At the foot of the Snežnik plateau, near the karst springs, a fortified castle was built in the 14th century to guard the passage through the Snežnik forests towards the Pivka Valley. The present-day Snežnik Castle is a well-preserved renaissance structure dating from the 17th century.

After 1857, when a railway link connected Ljubljana and Trieste via Rakek, Notranjska became a 'blind alley' and began to lag behind other regions. The Bloke plateau, which, according to Valvasor, was the center of Carniola, became a dead pocket; it has been revived only recently with a modern main road. The freeway, cutting through the woods of Notranjska, was also instrumental in bringing the towns and regions of Notranjska closer to central Slovenia.

6 The Rak stream has created a true parade of karst wonders in Rakov Škocjan: collapse caves, natural bridges, caves, and sources. Rakov Škocjan was protected by law in 1949.

7 The Postojna Cave won world fame as early as 1818 owing to its marvellous dripstone scenery, which is held to be among the most exquisite in the world. The cave system combines the once separate Postojna, Črna, Pivka, Magdalena, and Otoška jama caves. 21 km of passages have been researched, and 5 km are arranged for guided tours.

8 Predjama Castle, a fortified nest in front of a karst cave, has preserved its 16th-century Renaissance character. The cave behind it conceals the older (Jama) castle. A historical event from the latter half of the 15th century, when the castle was under siege for a long time, gave birth to the legend about the robber knight Erasmus of Predjama (Erasmus Luegger).

9 Bloke is a vast karst plateau on the Notranjska side of the Dinaric Karst, 10 km long and about 5 km wide. The biggest settlement is Nova vas. Bogs and marshy meadows (among the best preserved in Slovenia, fed by subterranean springs) with an interesting flora are spread along the Bloščica stream, which meanders across the northern part of the plateau. The Bloke skis belong to the area's ethnological heritage.

10 The Križna jama cave is fed by waters from the Bloke plateau, which flow down to the Cerknica polje. The entrance area of the cave is a rich site of cave bear bones. Deeper down the cave the water course is interrupted by sinter barriers, and this results in about 22 tiny lakes in the dry period. The water passages can be visited only by boat, with lights and a guide.

11 Snežnik Castle is first mentioned in historical sources in 1269. Through the centuries the castle changed owners several times, and for the last century its occupants owned the Snežnik forests. From 1868 to 1875 the castle housed the Slovene Forestry School. It is the only castle in Slovenia with furnishings from the late 19th century and is surrounded by an extensive park.

10

11

Stone and Vines

The Vipava Valley, the Trnovo Forest, Nanos, the Kras

1 Nanos is a vast karst plateau, located between the Postojna basin and the Vipava valley. Its southern and western slopes are steep, the plateau stretches out over an area that is 10 km long and reaches a height of 800 to 1,300 m. The high-altitude landscape is full of sink-holes, dry *dolines*, ice caves, caves, and pits. The view from the summit of Pleša captures the whole of south-western Slovenia. The southern and western slopes of Nanos are protected as a natural park because of the rare and interesting flora.

Left: The village Kobjeglava on the Kras plateau
Below: Location of aerial photograph shown on map 1 : 300 000

Central Slovenia communicates with Primorje (the Littoral) through two avenues: the valleys of the Soča and the Vipava, and via Postojna and Koper. Between the two lies the plateau of the Kras (the Karst, the Carso) inclined towards the Gulf of Trieste on the Italian side of the border.

The dividing line between the continental mountains and high plateaus, and the low-lying, sub-Mediterranean Vipava Valley, runs along the fringe peaks of Trnovski gozd (the Trnovo Forest) around Čaven. The peaks reach the 1,200-metre mark above sea level, while the bottom of the Vipava Valley is a mere 80 metres above sea level. The biogeographical borderline is sharper here than anywhere else in Slovenia. In several places, Dinaric fir and beech forests lie only a hundred metres from warmth-loving shrubbery, speckled with black beech and tiny ash trees. The two plant habitats are separated by a wind-ravaged, rocky strip overgrown with resistant, weather-hardened plants. The plant life of this region embraces several representatives of Alpine and Illyrian flora as well as some rare indigenous plants, such as *Hladnikia pastinacifolia*. The mountain top of Kucelj (1,237 m) provides a unique experience in this respect. Surrounded by edelweiss, we savor the view of the Vipava Valley, dotted with vineyards and quaint villages shaded by fig trees.

Despite a modest altitude (1,262 m), Nanos's Pleša ("The Bald Top" of Nanos) is a natural balcony with a view over the whole of south-western Slovenia. The vista reaches as far as Javorniki, Snežnik, and the Istrian mountains in Čičarija, spanning the entire Kras region as far as the Gulf of Trieste, and in clear weather, Friuli and Venice appear on the horizon.

The bottom of the Vipava Valley and the hilly terrain on its south-western fringes consist of flysch rock. This soft rock also contains layers of marl, sandstone, limestone breccia, and clay slate, deposited at the bottom of a Tertiary sea which covered the south-western part of Slovenia. Flysch of similar age and composition can also be found in the lower Pivka Valley and in the Reka basin, in the hinterland of Piran and Sečovlje, as well as in the Soča Valley and Goriška Brda. Suitable soil and a mild climate, marred only by a northerly winter wind, gave rise to agriculture, wine-making and, more recently, fruit growing. On the other side of the Vipava Valley is spread the undulating plateau of the Kras, which again is made up of limestone.

▶

2 The Trnovski gozd (Trnovo Forest) is a vast karst plateau, completely covered by forests. Its borders are the Čepovan valley to the west and Nanos to the east; to the south it rises steeply from the Vipava valley. Large karst sink-holes, closed on all sides, retain cold air, and the cold and warm layers of air are therefore reversed, and so are the vegetation belts. The best-known cold pole is Smrekova draga (in the photograph).The southern fringes of the plateau are protected as a landscape park because of their particular flora.

3 Vipava is an ancient settlement at the vigorous sources of the river of the same name, which is fed by the Nanos karst plateau.

4 Zemono, a Late Renaissance hunting mansion, has an arcaded corridor and rich wall paintings in the interior. It lies on a low hill in the middle of the Vipava valley.

5 Vipavski Križ, a cluster settlement on an elongated hill west of Ajdovščina, is a monument of urban architecture. The settlement flourished in the 16th century under the Attems family, when the preacher and best-known Slovene writer of the Baroque period, Janez Svetokriški (Tobia Lionelli) was active in the local Capuchin monastery.

6 Rihemberk Castle stands on a rounded hilltop above the settlement of Branik. The medieval 12th-century castle gradually developed into an extensive residence with Renaissance defence walls, cylindrical corner towers, and residential wings with Baroque elements. The Lanthieri family, the last owners, lived here until the Second World War. After the war the castle was blown up and has now been renovated considerably.

7 At Ajdovščina, the remains of the extensive late-Roman Castra can still be seen. The picture shows the best preserved round wall-tower, of which there were originally fourteen.

The landscape is called "the original Kras/Karst" because karst phenomena and natural processes on the limestone surface and underground were first described and scientifically explained in this part of Slovenia. The Kras stretches over an area of 500 km^2 between the lower Soča (Isonzo), the Gulf of Trieste, the Vipava Valley, Vremščica, Brkini and Slavnik. Only a small part of the area lies in Italy. The first Slovene cave opened to tourists was Vilenica, located between Sežana and the village of Lokev. It was well-known already in the 17th century. Today, the Škocjan Caves (Škocjanske jame) near Divača are more popular. They offer the most breath-taking scenes of the sculptural powers of nature: collapse dolines, a natural bridge, a waterfall, giant subterranean halls, and the longest subterranean canyon carved out by the River Reka, the sculptor of these wonders of the subterranean realm. The Škocjan Caves were listed in the 1986 UNESCO Register of Natural Heritage.

Thanks to its strategic location on the ancient trade route linking the northern Adriatic, the Eastern Alps, the Pannonian Plain and the western Balkans, the Vipava Valley played an important role even in the Late Stone Age. Iron Age outposts, forts, were perched high up on the flanks of the valley (such as at Planina nad Vipavo, Gradišče above Ajdovščina, and Sv. Danijel above Šempas). The Roman fort of Castra, on the site of present-day Ajdovščina, was set up when the Romans penetrated further east in the last century BC, and later became an administrative center of the Roman Military Borderland on the territory of Trnovski gozd and Hrušica, known as *Alpes Iuliae*. The fort also maintained a part of the vast system of defensive walls (*Claustra*) between Hrušica (*Ad Pirum*) and Vrhnika (*Nauportus*). In 394 Vrhpolje was the site of a key battle in the decline of Antiquity between the rival Roman Emperors Theodosius and Eugenius. Theodosius won, but this did not save the unity of the Roman Empire, which disintegrated in 395 into its eastern and western parts.

As in the Vipava Valley, old routes meandered through the Kras from the hinterland to the coast. On the edge of the Kras plateau, the strategic highpoint at the entrance to the Vipava Valley was crowned by a fortified settlement at Štanjel, which developed on the site of previous Iron Age and Roman settlements. Štanjel Castle is a Romanesque structure, with later Gothic and Renaissance additions leading in the 17th century to its present-day baroque appearance. At the foot of the Kras, on a hillock above the Branica Valley (Braniška dolina) rose the medieval Castle Rihemberk, with a characteristic round tower. The building of the southern railway line from Vienna to Trieste via Divača and Sežana brought new life to these two towns in 1857.

People faced the challenge of the Kras very early in human history. Traces of human presence in the area go back to the prehistoric period. Modest, yet fertile patches of karst soil produce excellent crops, such as the well-known *Teran* wine. The production of this wine, however, requires hard, manual labor. The main shortcoming of the region continues to be the water supply, which, despite abundant precipitation, sinks into the cavern-riddled ground. In the previous century, the denuded hay-making slopes and taluses were improved through reforestation with black pine. In the process, the landscape of the Kras has also changed and the risk of fire increased.

8 The medieval settlement of Štanjel (Gornja vas) nests on a hill and is tightly built-up on terraces, made of local stone, and surrounded by a wall. Typical elements are the tight rows of houses and the wells in open spaces. In the 1920s and 30s the architect Maks Fabiani designed the terraced Ferrari garden with a water reservoir, grotto, and viewpoint on the eastern edge of the hill. Štanjel was heavily damaged during the Second World War and is slowly restored to its formed appearance.

9 Among the thousands of known karst caves in Slovenia, the Škocjan caves occupy a unique place. The coexistence of cultural heritage (an archaeological site, art monuments) and natural sights made them the first Slovene sight to be registered on UNESCO's list of world heritage in 1986; later, the caves and their environs were declared a regional park. The Skočjan caves feature among others the deepest known subterranean canyon, carved out by the Reka river. The river enters the underground below the village of Škocjan.

10 These pan-shaped forms in the Škocjan caves are created by the water flow.

11 The climate of the Kras was found to be favourable for horse breeding as early as the 16th century. In 1580 the Lipica stud farm was established near Sežana. For centuries it belonged to the Austrian Imperial Court. It is world famous as a stud farm for breeding autochthonous Lippizaner horses.

12 The Kras is the home of Teran, a one-year old red wine with the typical sour-bitterish flavor. The vines thrive on a limited area of red karst soil *(terra rossa)*. In the photograph, the vineyards near Tomaj have donned the rich colours of autumn.

13 The village architecture of the Kras is enticing because of its variety and inventive solutions. This house in Kobdilj features a typical *spahnjenica*: the fireplace and chimney built as an extension.

14 The present-day Botanical Garden is based on a garden with a romantic design, laid out next to a villa in Sežana in the 19th century. It has a beautiful park area and many interesting plants, and has been protected by law since 1950.

15 The Vilenica is the oldest tourist cave in Slovenia and the world. Rules for visiting the cave date from 1633.

12

13
14

15

The Coast and its Hinterland

The Brkini, the Materija Valley, Slavnik, the Littoral

1 The Matarsko (or Podgrajsko) podolje (the Materija or Podgrad valley) between Kozina and Starod consists of little more than caves, sink-holes, stretches of barren stony ground, and overgrowing pastures. The best-known cave is the Dimnice cave near Markovščina (in the photograph is the entrance to the cave).

Left: The Piran peninsula
Below: Location of aerial photograph shown on map 1 : 300 000

The former province of Carniola, whose borders were in place until the Napoleonic wars, bordered the coast on the Gulf of Trieste between Štivan and Trieste and on the eastern Istrian coast in the Kvarner Bay. More recent history assigned to the Republic of Slovenia that part of the coast in north-western Istria, which since antiquity has been settled by a Romance population. However, in the so-called Trieste corridor between Štivan and Barkovlje, numerous Slovene settlements remained, which after 1954 were assigned to Italy. The new border meant that the Istrian cities of Koper, Izola and Piran were cut off from the Kras and the rest of Slovenia. Thus, a new road had to be built from Senožeče via Divača and Črni Kal to the intersection below Škofije. The construction was completed in 1957. Another connection was established in 1967, when the railway line joined the old Istrian railway at Prešnica, thus providing ties with the hinterland for the Koper port.

The Slovene littoral is not a unified geographic area. The national border cuts transversely through natural geographical units. The easternmost hilly range of flysch rock, Brkini, indented by numerous ravines and gullies, borders Notranjska. The streams from the northern and eastern slopes feed the Reka (flowing through Notranjska and Brkini) which then sinks into the Škocjan Caves and feeds the sources of the Brojnica and the Timav in the Gulf of Trieste. From the south-western slopes, the water has only a short run before it reaches the limestone strata of the valley floor, the Materija Valley, and sinks. It probably recedes underground into the Kvarner Bay. The Materija Valley (Matarsko podolje, also called Podgrajsko podolje) provides a suitable passage for the old road between Trieste and Rijeka. Further to the west, the limestone territory rises into the ridge of Čičarija, with Slavnik (1,028 m) as its highest peak, and then descends again and levels out in the Podgorski Kras of sink holes at an altitude of 400 metres. Behind the villages of Socerb, Kastelec and Črnotiče, the Kras plateau suddenly breaks off, forming a picturesque wall from Osp via Črni Kal to Podpeč, and further into Istria. It ultimately sinks towards the flysch valleys of the Osapska Reka and the Rižana. This is where Primorje proper (the Littoral) begins and where, in sun-kissed and sheltered areas, magnificent Mediterranean fruit trees grow.

The soft flysch of the coastal region is at first glance somewhat less attractive than the white limestone, but the region does have some distinctive features. The mouth of the Dragonja at Sečovlje was a salt works as early as in the Roman period. The vast surface of shallow water is a true Eden for water

2 The settlements along the Brkini range are scattered both sides of the ridge between the stony bottom of the Materija valley and the Reka valley. Compared to the poor karst soil, the flysch soil of the Brkini is much more favourable for agriculture.

3 Črni Kal, a village below the Kraški rob
4 (the Karst's Edge), is not only famous because of its slanted tower, but it also has the oldest known peasant house in Slovenia – confirmed by an inscription and the date 1489 cut into stone. The rapid transition from the continental Kras to the milder climate of the flysch-covered coast is quite evident. Rare species of plants and animals have their habitats in the rocks above the village.

fowl, and a necessary stop-over on their autumn and spring migrations. On the Strunjan Peninsula, a chunk of the coast has been left intact. It is bound by an 80-metre high cliff, the most extensive flysch cliff on the entire Adriatic coast. Preparations are under way to declare Strunjan's *Mesečev zaliv* (Moon Bay) a nature reserve.

The Slovene littoral has been influenced by Mediterranean culture. The sites of today's cities were perhaps already colonized in the time of ancient Greeks, and were full-fledged cities by the Roman period: Piranum (Piran), Haliaetum (Simonov zaliv, near Izola), and Aegida or Capris (Koper). The settlements continued into the early Middle Ages, when the townships were for a short time included within Byzantine Istria and were later part of the Frankish Empire. They then gradually came under the jurisdiction of the Venetian Republic, where they remained until the end of 1797. After brief periods under Austrian and French rule, they again became part of the Austrian Empire until its dissolution in 1918. Under Venice, the development of towns was hindered by the Venetian metropolis itself, and under the Austrians, because of the proximity of Trieste (which was privileged by having a railway connection with Vienna). As a modest substitute for a supporting role, a narrow-gauge railway was built in 1902 between Trieste and Poreč, which operated until 1936. Italian rule over the territory in the period between the two wars (1918–1943) did not change its subordinate role vis-a-vis Trieste. The economy of the three towns was mainly dependent on salt production and fishing, which, however, did not permit any greater development. The most favourable period in terms of economic prosperity was under Venetian rule, when the Adriatic republic had a monopoly and Austria had no other access to salt. This period gave rise to many stories about salt smuggling (Martin Krpan being a famous example). When the present border once again severed the port of Trieste from the Slovene hinterland, its role was assumed by Koper, which quickly became Slovenia's largest port.

Economic stagnation under Austria and Italy also meant that the three coastal cities maintained their medieval appearance, with the church on a central elevation, narrow streets and a main square; small, sheltered ports, so-called *mandrači*, such as the ancient core of Piran, are particularly notable.

Economic development after the Second World War also brought some undesirable consequences. Rapid growth and at times inappropriate architecture greatly affected the medieval appearance of Koper, Izola somewhat less, while Piran was spared. When after WW2 a large proportion of the Italian population left the coastal cities and Istria, the loss of cultural and national identity became a real threat. Slovenia and Italy, however, work together to recreate an atmosphere of tolerance, where the bilingual community could forge ties with the community living across the border.

5 St. George's at Piran: on a wall of the Baptistery dedicated to St. John the Baptist is a branch-crucifix with the Corpus Christi, dating from 1310 (Venetian workshop).

6 The present-day village of Socerb occupies the site of a prehistoric hillfort. Here, the Romans built a fortress, and in the Middle Ages a fortified castle was erected. For many centuries the castle guarded the border between Austrian Carniola and Venetian Istria. Its wall offers a splendid view of Dolina, Boljunec, and Trieste. The well-known Sveta jama (Holy Cave) is quite near; according to the legend it was the dwelling of the Trieste martyr St. Servulus, who was killed in 284.

7 Koper developed into a big sea port with Slovenia and Central Europe as its hinterland only after it was incorporated into Slovenia.

8 The famous small church of the Holy Trinity in Hrastovlje stands in the headwater region of the Rižana. It is a Romanesque, three-nave church from the 12th and 13th centuries. The church is surrounded by a defence wall from the period of the Turkish incursions.

9 The interior of the Hrastovlje church is decorated with expressive narrative Gothic frescoes from the 15th century, among them the famous *Dance of Death* (the photograph shows a part of the paintings).

10 The Gothic Loggia of Koper stands at the main square, across the Praetorian Palace; it was built in 1462.

11 Koper's cathedral of the Assumption can pride itself on numerous works of art, among others an exceptional painting by Vittore Carpaccio – *The Enthroned Madonna*.

10

11

12 Unlike Koper, Piran has managed to preserve its medieval appearance intact. Together with nearby Portorož it is the most attractive seaside holiday resort of north Istria.

13 Only a small stretch section of the Slovenia's short sea shore on the Strunjan peninsula has preserved its natural condition. These remains of a wild flysch shore are now a natural park.

14 Many genuinely Mediterranean plant species, which are very rare elsewhere in Slovenia, grow on the Stena hill, a small limestone hump in the Dragonja valley. Stena is a natural monument. Its most impressive feature is a limestone overhang.

15 Portorož is Slovenia's leading seaside and health resort with numerous hotels and private rooms and apartments.

16 Koštabona above the Dragonja valley is a typical Istrian settlement on a rock promontory in the southern area of the Šavrin (Koper) hills, in which narrow streets wind their way around clustered houses. Set on the hilltops of Istria, the villages were safe from invaders as well as land slides.

17 The Sečovlje saltworks are converted marshes. For centuries saltworkers constructed channels, dams, and salt fields. This ancient procedure of extracting salt has been preserved into the present, but is slowly becoming extinct. Today, the saltpans are a natural park where halophytes grow, and home to many species of water birds. A small saltworks museum introduces us to the past.

Pp. 124, 125: The saltpans of Sečovlje

16

17

123

Picture Credits

The name of the photographer (or that of the copyright holder) is followed by the number of page and – in brackets – by the consecutive number of picture. AMK = The Archives of the Založba Mladinska knjiga Publishing House

The Lipica Archives 114 (11); The Postojna Cave Archives 108 (7); The Terme Čatež (the Čatež Spa) Archives 85 (9); Dragan Arrigler 78 (10); Andrej Blatnik 54 (4), 123 (17); Virgilij Dariš 44 (5), 46 (7); Damjan Gale 79 (12); Geodetski zavod Slovenije 6, 12, 18, 26, 34, 42, 48, 52, 58, 66, 74, 80, 86, 92, 98, 104, 110, 116, plus the frontispiece map and the aerial photographs location maps; Janez Gregori 19 (1), 20 (2), 111 (1); Jože Hanc – AMK 4, 9 (7), 11 (13), 14 (3, 6), 15 (7), 16 (9, 12), 17 (13, 14, 15), 22 (10), 24 (15, 16, 17), 40 (15), 41 (17, 18), 45 (6), 47 (12, 13), 50 (5), 51 (7), 54 (3), 56 (8), 63 (12), 64 (15), 65 (18), 76 (3, 5), 77 (6), 78 (7), 82 (2, 4), 84 (7), 85 (10), 87 (1), 88 (3, 4, 5, 7), 89 (8), 90 (10), 91 (12, 13, 15), 93 (1), 95 (6), 101 (6), 102 (7, 8, 10), 103 (11), 105 (1), 106 (2, 3), 107 (5), 108 (6, 8, 9), 109 (11), 112 (3, 4, 5, 6), 114 (8), 115 (13), 118 (3, 4), 119 (5), 120 (6, 8), 122 (12), 123 (16), 126; Jože Hanc 21 (6), 82 (3), 83 (5), 122 (13); Samo Jenčič 54 (5), 57 (12); Matjaž Jež 53 (1), 76 (4); Bogdan Kladnik 20 (4), 23 (11), 32 (13), 96 (10), 109 (10), 115 (15), 117 (1); Lado Klar 68 (5), 70 (9, 12), 72 (14); Stane Klemenc – AMK 7 (1), 10 (8, 9), 16 (8), 24 (13), 25 (18), 43 (1), 60 (2), 67 (1), 71 (13), 73 (18), 75 (1), 76 (2), 78 (9), 96 (7, 8, 9), 97 (12), 101 (5), 103 (12), 114 (10); Stane Klemenc 8 (2, 4, 5), 10 (10), 11 (12), 20 (5), 22 (8), 24 (14), 25 (19), 27 (1), 28 (2, 3), 29 (5), 30 (6, 7, 8), 31 (10), 32 (12, 14, 15), 33 (17), 35 (1), 36 (2, 3, 4), 37 (5), 38 (8, 9), 39 (11, 12), 40 (14), 50 (2), 51 (8), 60 (3), 61 (7), 64 (14), 65 (17), 68 (4, 6), 70 (10, 11), 73 (19), 81 (1), 84 (6), 91 (14), 100 (3), 114 (9), 118 (2), 124–125; Miško Kranjec 68 (2); Marjan Krušič – AMK 13 (1), 14 (2), 16 (11), 38 (6, 10), 40 (13), 41 (16), 44 (4), 46 (9, 10, 11), 50 (3, 4, 6), 57 (13), 60 (5), 62 (8), 69 (7), 79 (11), 88 (6), 94 (2, 4), 95 (5), 96 (11), 100 (2), 112 (2), 113 (7), 115 (14); Marjan Krušič 22 (9), 31 (9), 32 (11); Siena Krušič – AMK 8 (3); Matevž Lenarčič 10 (11), 14 (5), 20 (3), 38 (7), 49 (1), 56 (7), 59 (1), 62 (11), 78 (8), 79 (13), 120 (7), 122 (15); Marjan Malej 33 (16); Nino Mihalek 10 (10); Janez Mikuž – AMK 46 (8), 57 (11), 60 (4), 61 (6), 62 (9), 62 (10); Janez Mikuž 64 (13); Peter Petru 85 (8); Luka Pintar 14 (4), 56 (10), 100 (4), 102 (9); Rafael Podobnik 115 (12); Jože Pojbič – AMK 68 (3); Jože Pojbič 56 (9), 70 (8), 72 (15, 16, 17), 97 (14); Janez Pukšič – AMK 99 (1); Janez Pukšič 55 (6); Peter Skoberne 22 (7), 28 (4), 44 (2), 122 (14); Marjan Smerke 8 (6), 23 (12), 54 (2), 88 (2), 90 (11), 120 (9), 121 (11); Janez Zrnec 16 (10), 44 (3), 90 (9), 94 (3), 97 (13), 106 (4); Gojko Zupan 121 (10); Joco Žnidaršič 64 (16)

Left: Dolenjska landscape

Greetings from Slovenia

Chapters on the regions of Slovenia: Stane Peterlin with Davorin Vuga

Editor's Foreword, Profile of Slovenia: Marjan Krušič

Photographs and Maps: see Picture Credits

English translation: Marjan Golobič

English language editing: Stanko Klinar

English language advisor: Philip Burt

Lay-out: Metka Žerovnik

Editor: Marjan Krušič

Published by Založba Mladinska knjiga, Ljubljana 2005

Managing Director: Milan Matos

Publishing Division, Executive Director: Bojan Kuhar

© Mladinska knjiga Založba, d. d., Ljubljana, 1991—2005

Printed by: MA–TISK, d. d., Maribor, 2005

Information on books by Publishing House Mladinska knjiga available
on the internet – http://www.emka.si

CIP - Kataložni zapis o publikaciji
Narodna in univerzitetna knjižnica, Ljubljana

908(497.4)
779:908(497.4)

PETERLIN, Stane
Greetings from Slovenia / [chapters on the regions of Slovenia Stane Peterlin with Davorin
Vuga ; editor's foreword, Profile of Slovenia Marjan Krušič ; English translation Marjan
Golobič]. - New ed. - Ljubljana : Mladinska knjiga, 2005

Prevod dela: Pozdravljena, Slovenija

ISBN 86-11-16362-1

1. Gl. stv. nasl. 2. Vuga, Davorin
123205888